Road to Oprah

John
&
Elaine

I pray for
continued peace
and blessings
on your journey
of life

Raymond Goode

Road to Oprah
Copyright © 2011 Raymond Goode
Published by: Raymond Goode

ISBN-978-1-61364-485-0

DEDICATION

I know my journey of life would not have been possible if wasn't for my mother constantly scraping her knees to pray for me. This journey, as well as my life is a complete dedication to the person who has made me smile when I was sad, laugh when I cried and comforted me during my times of pain. I draw my inspiration and strength from watching her. I truly understand the words to Marvin Sapp's, "Never would have made it" because that's how I feel about my mother, Lynette Goode. I never would have made it without you mom.

Letter to my mom:

Thank you for being the person that you are. I know that my life has always kept you on the edge of your seat but you have always known that I was special. You have always known the right words to say at the right time. Your words are powerful which separates you from all the other mothers of the world. I am proud to be who I am because you have always let me be who I am supposed to be. I will honor your name in the highest regards. Honesty, Courage, Strength, Endurance, Compassion, Integrity and Respect are all the qualities that you have instilled in me and I promise to show that to the world. The highest honor I have ever received is people calling me a momma's boy. Proudly, I am your son and you are my mother.

I love you mom

Thank You

Welcome to *Road to Oprah*

ACKNOWLEDGEMENT

To the World- I would like to thank each and every person that has bought a book, clicked on my Youtube videos or encouraged me to continue on my journey. I pray that my life's testimony has been an inspiration to each and every one of your lives. Every person that I have held a conversation with, I pray that I have motivated you to believe in a dream. Your dreams are the reason why I continuously follow mine.

Kim B.L.U.N.T- Thank you for the knowledge that you have given me. You were the finishing touch that I needed to grow. Whenever anything is needed, don't fail to call. I will show love.

Robert Townes- I can never give you enough praise. Your forewords are the amazing finishing touch needed to take my books to a whole other level. You've always kept it real and saw the real Raymond Goode. You turned me on to Nas who remains my favorite rapper to this day. You have shown me real friendship in immeasurable ways. I truly value the brotherhood that we have.

Vernal Coleman (Style Weekly), Marlene Jones (The Voice), Cesca Waterfield (Urbanviews Weekly) - Thank you all for the articles that you have featured on me. You three saw something in me that was interesting enough to report on. I will always give you exclusives when I come to the city.

The Squad- *Disclaimer: I apologize in advance if I have left anyone out. It was not intentional and my heart is with each and every one of you.*

Tyrell - Thanks for the studio time. We are going to take it back to Heineken and hot peppers. Eric - Better days are coming…I promise you that. Ernest - We will always be family. Tyrone (Face) - Love you in the heart. That will never change. Will (Corleone) - Keep it gutter. Stay on your path. Matthew - Stay up…my man…you already know what it is. Jamarl - Keep cutting those heads. You always keep me tight when I don't have the funds. We're family no matter how distant we are. Ty and Twan - still the craziest brothers I know. Joey - I always got your back. Thanks for all the rides to the gym. Bilal - I need more tattoos (in my incredible hulk voice). Keith - Family since day one…you know that. Travis -When you come home you won't have to worry about anything. William - Play your hand to the fullest. 30th platoon (Army boot camp) - I still got my fingers twisted and representing to the fullest. Scorpio/Whitaker, Blaze/McClain, Diamond/Hollins, Love, Muse, Tappin, Wisdom/Shea, Bailey, Cross, A-Z, Grey, Bradley, Nino, Nunez, The Duece, Q, Clarke A.K.A Mrs. Bradley, Ash, - You cats helped me to be me in your own ways. I will never forget the times that we shared and will always remember the times that we had together. The Army and Navy was some of the best times of my life. There are a whole lot of names that I'm forgetting but if you have a memory tied to me please forgive me for my forgetfulness and charge it to my brain and not my heart. Roney -Thank you for all the videos that you have helped me with. Your turnaround time and expertise is well noted. Marquis - Thank you for being one of the driving forces for putting my commercials together. You are definitely one of the people who assisted me with my vision. I see your hustle and I respect that. Clarence (Myles) - Keep pushing…my number is always open to you. John - Thank you for every cover that you have designed for my books. Money is absolutely priceless compared to what you have done for me. T.J. (Google) -You know half of my projects wouldn't be possible without you. Stay grinding homie. I'm right there for you when it's needed or wanted. You know that. Jacob - Thank for all the "Special Haircuts." You have respected my spiritual views and vice versa without being judgmental. Get your bags ready because where I go you will go. Antonio (Handz) - You already know the friendship that we have. You will be my personal bodyguard or at least I will keep you working. That's a promise. The way you knock people out, I might have to be the one to take you down myself. To my Haitian sensation, Wan Dral - You know we are going to party as soon as I get this jumping. Let's see the world. Coakley (Mish) - Thank you for your professionalism with the commercial. You are truly an art at your craft. Don't worry I'm going to be a springboard for you to reach your destiny. Dale - I'm proud of you booooy. Keep pushing and I will be there for you. I see growth and maturity in you and I'm enjoying watching you grow. Vincent - No matter where you're at we're still homies. You showed me how to get in trouble and I haven't been able to stop since.

Bianca - You continuously stick by my side even though you know I am absolutely crazy. I appreciate every night that you've spent editing my book. Don't worry about the world; I always got your back. The play and pause effect that you added to *Road to Oprah* was INGENIOUS. That was the final touch that gave this book the extra boost that was needed.

Justin (Q) - You get your own spot. When you touch down I guarantee that you will never see another cell again. I truly learned about loyalty from you. You are family no matter where you are. Around here you are a true Goode and I'm going to make sure you have it all when you come home. First of all, we're going to start with some fresh shades.

Deirdre Jones -Woooow…What you did for my first video (Great Pursuit) is a true blessing. I am grateful from the bottom of my heart. It was a masterpiece and even though I have never met you, thank you for seeing my vision the way your heart chose to see it.

Shaunda Davis - You've stuck with me through thick and thin and held tight to be one of the greatest friends that I've ever had. Thank you for your friendship and that comes from the bottom of my heart. I will always be there for you in any shape or form.

Syreeta (Bird) - My far away friend. Some things I still aint forgave myself for. You will always have a special place and you know why. I love you and I will come to Texas soon just give me some more time.

Katrina - You put a lot of time and patience in the *Traces of You* website. I appreciate your obsession of making sure everything is right to your likings. Your perfectionist attitude will carry you far and I am appreciative of the expertise that you committed to *www.tracesofyou.org*.

Daneka - As long as the blood is blue in the vein you will always be family. Nothing can ever change that. I love you.

To the Kids - Thank you for allowing me to be an inspiration to your lives. I know that each and every one of you has a destiny that needs to be fulfilled; I pray that I can assist you with achieving that dream. Believe in your dream and all is conquerable. I will never give up on you because people have never given up on me. I believe in each and every one of you and I will give my all to prove that.

To Oprah - My life has been riddled with hardships, trials and tribulations. You have given me what no one has been able to, Focus. I am a better person because of your inner spirit.

My family - You all continuously hold me down in your own ways. I appreciate you all for letting me be me and backing me in all that I do. To see your name, refer back to *Traces of You*; however, I must give a shot out to Jabari Cox and Marilyn Payne/Perry since I forgot your names in the last book. Now y'all can get off my back (ha-ha).

Last but not least - I would like to thank the higher powers that be who have given me strength to push forward. My faith is strong and I pray that I will continue to have the endurance to endure, the strength to stay strong and the wisdom to educate. My ancestors and forefathers have taught me to put my best foot forward and help as many people as I can. I will live the dreams of my ancestors and never forget that one of the truest values of life is people helping people. It is my ancestor's blood that is running through my veins and I do not intend to disappoint.

TABLE OF CONTENTS

Foreword…………………………………………………………………….8

Introduction of Author…………………………………………………...9

Preface/How it all started…..…………………………………………….10

Chapter 1…………….....................December………………………………12

Chapter 2…………………………January………………………………16

Chapter 3…………………………February………………………………45

Chapter 4…………………………March………………………………60

Chapter 5…………………………April………………………………94

Chapter 6…………………………..May………………………………...126

Traces of Raymond Goode…………………………………………………156

FOREWORD

The foundation associated with human existence embodies theoretical principles that define control as a calculated action which facilitates order, promotes balance, and establishes a false sense of power. Our social structure is designed to enforce stability and create control by exhausting an endless amount of resources. Control produces a false sense of empowerment by imposing a list of rules that restrict or promote behavior deemed acceptable by the majority. Government organizations enact laws, employers implement corporate policies, couples form relational boundaries, parents establish adolescent curfews, and educational institutions design mandates in an effort to promote long-lasting control.

Everyone strives to obtain a certain level of control. Some may even say that developing measures that enforce control allow individuals to experience provisional solidarity. Nevertheless, the purest form of control is an uncontrollable substance because; that which can not be controlled is the control within itself. Many people fear an uncontrollable substance. Society views an uncontrollable substance as unpredictable, unreliable, and disorganized. However, the erratic nature of an uncontrollable substance is the foundational basis that defines purpose and establishes direction.

The philosophical premise associated with an uncontrollable substance involves the ability to exist without boundaries, limitations, or self imposed restrictions. Road to Oprah documents how an impulsive excursion transitioned into one man's destiny. Raymond Goode's journey demonstrates how the capricious nature of an uncontrollable substance can evolve into a cohesive set of circumstances that establish stability as he embarks on a Road to Oprah.

Robert

INTRODUCTION OF THE AUTHOR

As an adolescent growing up Raymond Goode wasn't the most popular kid; he experienced the pitfalls of not belonging. Despite his formidable years he was always told he would one day be destined for greatness. During his senior year, he developed into an urbane young man. At that pivotal time he met his first love which fueled his then unknown propensity to write. It began with the playful exchange of a letter between two young lovers during class; which graduated to notebooks full of stories about his love. After the breakup of his first love, Raymond found solace in writing.

As an adult, he found himself in yet another turbulent breakup. This time however, led him spiraling deep into depression and ultimately attempting to end his life. Even through his pain he chose to write letters to express the hurt he couldn't verbalize. In the midst of writing his farewell letters, he knew it was not yet his time. From the darkness came light, he returned to what provided him peace, writing. He finally realized what he was destined to do; from this the *Traces of You* project was born.

Raymond Goode, the author of *Traces of You* presents his second literary work *Road to Oprah*.

Road to Oprah is a continuing journey of the *Traces of You* project. This book was written to keep the stories alive of the fifty random individuals who candidly allowed him into their thoughts. Raymond Goode has vowed to share their stories with the world. The Oprah Winfrey show was the medium he chose. Although he has never viewed the show, he connects with Oprah as a humanitarian. He left familiarity to keep his promise and traveled to Chicago, Illinois knowing no one; living homeless and surviving off instinct. Road to Oprah delves into the psyche of the author, Raymond Goode, stripping away his exterior and allowing the reader to understand Raymond.

In the author's words, "The world will criticize you, so find who you are and remember to be yourself." Through his eyes on the *Road to Oprah* you may find *Traces of You*...

Shaunda Davis

HOW IT ALL STARTED.....

I should have started this documentary a long time ago like my mother suggested but I suppose better late than ever. My book idea (Traces of You) started around the middle of last year (2010 to be specific). The idea came from a female I was dating (Nicole) or rather we had just broken up. Nicole was out of the country and even though we had broken up she still had a tremendous hold on my heart. I was in the club one night and I saw this guy walking around selling roses. Nicole is a feminist revolutionary kind of woman. She is the kind of woman that is turned on by books rather than flowers. So, I began to think that in order to impress Nicole he would have to walk around selling books like Marcus Garvey, Assatta Shakur, Malcolm X and authors of that nature.

I listened to the rap music that was playing and knew that she would rather listen to artist such as the Roots, Bilal, Erykah Badu, Blackstar, etc. My brain dwelled on the fact that since she wasn't such a conventional female then she would not want an expensive ring but something rather from the heart. Then something hit me. I wondered how many people had different answers and ways that they would like to be proposed to or do a marriage proposal. Even though I was highly intoxicated my brain was on fire. As I drove home that night I came up with a list of questions which began the birth of *Traces of You*. Now we can fast forward some.

I have had a lot of comments (positive and negative) on the move that I chose to make. The word that circulates the best is 'crazy' when people describe me or my movement (I actually kind of like that word because it means that I'm different from most people). A good friend of mine (Joey) told me a long time ago that when people love me they really love me and when they hate me they really hate me (That's very true to this day). My family and friends thought that my decision to leave December 31st was erratic behavior since I was leaving two jobs and my own house which at this time I would like to thank Medicaid. I know I was one of the few people in the field of counseling who had no degree whatsoever but still had the privilege of working with kids. I was able to maintain positions such as an In-home Counselor, Juvenile Corrections Officer, and Senior Recreational Counselor. A lot of these jobs I acquired through any means necessary but I refuse to indulge any further because a few of my friends are still in the struggle and I refuse to sell them out for fame or money. Furthermore, I would like to give Medicaid a great bow because besides the money working with kids is the most rewarding experience a person can have. To change the possible negative outcome of a child is one of the greatest and most rewarding experiences that I could ever have encountered in my life. There are reasons why I chose to not go back in the workforce. For one, with no degree I could never attain a job again. For two, the mission that I'm embarking will inspire children on a global scale.

As December 31st approached and my brain began to venture out on how I can make this project more exciting I came up with the idea of making audio c.d. books. That idea mainly came from my dad. I can remember when we were young my mom used to read the caption at the bottom of the TV screen. It seemed pretty normal to me until I realized later in life that my dad couldn't read. Don't take that out of context because his inability to read boosted his other qualities. He has been and is still custodial supervisor at the school that he works for. He is a hustler and has always been doing side jobs such as tree work, trash collecting, metal scrapping and whatever side hustle he could do so we could afford three vehicles, a three bedroom house, and whatever else was needed. I know that his inability to read has stifled him from fulfilling a lot of his goals and dreams, so I came up with the idea of audio c.d. books. I needed for him to hear my work.

My documentaries on Youtube are for the children to keep track of my progress. I need for children to know that dreams are still worth dreaming and sometimes to achieve those dreams a person has to be willing to give up everything in order to succeed. As the saying goes, "In order to learn how to swim you can't just test the water but instead dive right in." In my mind, I truly believe that a person selling drugs, prostituting, or quitting school is 'crazy.' To me, what I'm doing is actually pretty sane. In my mind when the kids start griping and moaning about the things that they don't have or a task that they can't complete they can click on my videos and be encouraged. I pray that if they can see my plight then it would make their challenges less challenging.

What the reader must understand is that this trip is completely for the kids; nothing more - nothing less. As December 31st approaches I began to create a buzz for myself. I started letting people hear my audio c.d. book which is really scary because now I was starting to let people in on my creativity and allowing them to judge my work. When my article came out in the Richmond VOICE, local free newspaper (thanks to Marlene for showing interest), that began to garner attention in the Richmond, Virginia area. I felt like if I can't create a buzz in my own hometown then I should not be leaving at all. People began to take notice and even though I was still called 'crazy' I began to hear words such as inspirational, awe, and amazement.

I didn't have a lot of emotions leading up to my departure date. I didn't know how to feel about my trip but it was something that needed to be done…plain and simple. People shed tears for my departure but emotionally I couldn't. I tried to explain that this was not the life I chose. I have been engaged twice, served in the army and navy, and held numerous of jobs…but this was the life that chose me. I tried to make my own path instead of allowing the path to choose my footsteps. I'm destined for greatness and my life shows it each and every way. My entire life people have told me that there is a mark on my life. I have been told that I am going to be a preacher or that I'm running from something. I tell people that I can't possibly run from anything but I am running towards something. Well here you have it folks…I have stripped everything away from me and will step out on faith to see if I really possess this mark that everyone says I have. If everything that people say about me is true then we will find out together. Let's find out what faith really is. We are going to find out together.

Chapter 1

December

December 31st

Out with the old; in with the new. I now know what that phrase means. I get tired of people making New Year's Eve resolutions and not sticking to them. People say all the time they are going to give up smoking knowing that they won't and two weeks later they're back to puffing away. *Pause: I really do need to stop smoking because it is a bad habit but the reason why they are bad is because I like them (ha-ha). Play:* I chose this date because I couldn't change my mind. I had planned to leave at 12pm but with my family nothing is ever on time. I spent the majority of the morning with my mother and sister. Nothing fancy; we just ate the food that I had to buy. *Pause: Imagine that. I'm leaving and I still have to buy the food (ha-ha gotta love my family). Play:* I saw my brother and he gave me a hug. *Pause: Woooow...a hug from my brother? Play:* Now, that was big for me because he is not one to show a lot of affection. I saw a few friends, Bianca and Jewell *(see...I mentioned y'all names).* They have been a great help in this journey. They both cried and wished me well.

I drove off listening to Nas and R. Kelly's, "Street Dreamer" remix. That song always makes me feel elevated and puts my mind on another level. As I looked in my rearview mirror it felt as though my problems in Virginia were the problems in Virginia. I knew that there was going to be a whole new set of problems that I would have to face.

The first stop I made was Pittsburgh. There was no way possible I was going to travel and not party for New Year's Eve. Pittsburgh was a whole new feeling for me since I was traveling alone. They had a huge party on the streets. There was a flame throwing lady who swallowed fire and they had a free nightclub where there was a live salsa band. The woman singing was amazing. This was not anything that you would see in Virginia. Randomly, two white women stopped me and asked to take a picture of my haircut. *Pause: I like to get waves cut into my hair which is a new style for me. I believe black people should use their hair as a way of expressing themselves. It is a way for me to express my freedom from the stereotypes of what a black male is supposed to look like. Play:* As I continued to walk, I saw an old school band. I'm so sorry I forgot their name, but they were really good. The streets were packed with people and everyone was having a good time. Something that really stuck out in my head was that they had their own ball drop. For some reason I did not want to see it drop and turned to walk away as they were doing the countdown. No particular reason why but I didn't want to see it fall. As I was walking away I saw the reflection of the fireworks in the glass in front of me…that was a sight and a sign for me. I instantly thought of Drake's song, "Fireworks." It's like I saw the fame in my eyes and what was predestined for me. Even though I felt as though I didn't know the direction I was taking, all I knew was that I was being pulled and I was tired of resisting.

As I continued walking, I began talking to two white guys who were friendly enough to shoot a "Traces of You" documentary with me. The dude was way too excited about shooting my video but we had a good time. They even offered me a slice of pizza because they owned the pizza shop on the corner. Then, I sparked a conversation with a tour bus driver who offered me a free ride to the Pittsburgh Steelers stadium. *Pause: Now there was no way I was going to come all the way here and not show love to my Uncle Tony's favorite team. Play:* It was my first time viewing a NFL stadium. I couldn't go in but I loved just being in the vicinity to shoot a documentary.

Even though it was New Year's Eve I hadn't had a drink yet so I walked across the street to the local TGIF and got a drink. This white guy walked over and sparked up a conversation with me and even bought me a drink. I know that it is a Steelers town so I asked him if everyone had to be a Steelers fan. He told me that if you weren't a Steelers fan already the longer you stayed in Pittsburgh the greater your chances of being converted. I say to this day "Gooooo Redskins!" I left from there and since I didn't have a ride back to my car I had to walk.

It was a beautiful night so I really didn't mind walking. I spotted the baseball stadium and a crazy idea popped into my head. I decided to jump the fence and shoot a documentary in the park. *Pause: Alcohol has a strange effect on people. It makes you do things that a sober person wouldn't think of doing. I didn't even think of the steel nails protruding on the very top of the fence. Play:* I began to climb and I stepped on a nail. That nail went through my shoe and halfway through my foot. I didn't initially feel the pain but jumped down immediately. As I walked away I just knew that there was probably someone in a guard shack somewhere laughing at all the stupid drunk people that attempted this feat. This was the first quick rule that I learned. *Rule #1:* I have to always take care of myself because it's only me and there would be no one to call on for assistance when I faced a problem. I had to walk about twelve blocks back to the car with blood oozing out of my foot. The alcohol was still in my system which is a good thing because I still did not feel the pain. I finally made it back to the car but couldn't drive because I promised my niece that I would not drive intoxicated. *Pause: Now that's a strong dilemma. Look for emergency care or keep a promise to my niece. I chose to keep my promise because my word is my bond. Play:* I went to sleep in my car but when I woke up three hours later…DAMN…the pain was unimaginable. I knew it was hospital time because the alcohol had worn off and the pain had finally sunk in.

I found out that the V.A. hospital was in the area and took my butt there a.s.a.p. That night (or day rather) I woke up in the hospital. I can't say how I feel about the situation but I was happy to be waking up in a bed (ha-ha). As a matter of fact, I went back to sleep for a couple of more hours. *Pause: It is nice to have the benefits of the military, even though I had been kicked out of the army and navy. I survived in both branches long enough that I could continue to claim my veteran status. Play:* I left Pittsburgh with new documentaries, a new memory, and crutches and continued to drive west. The pain was so bad sometimes that I had to control the pedals of my car with my left foot and elevate my right one in the passenger seat. This was not an easy task ladies and gentleman, but I was on the right path and one thing that I have to admit is that I was on the right path. I would have never experienced any of those things had I stayed in Virginia.

Chapter 2

Nothing stays the same forever but the willpower to endure the task until the end is the true miracle.

January

January 1st

Indiana Babyyyy...Notre Dame...I know absolutely nothing about Notre Dame but I do remember that movie Rudy (which was actually a good movie). So, I decided that I should stop when I saw the sign on the highway. I stopped and took pictures of the basketball stadium (which was still hard to do since I was still on crutches). I met this guy who was walking past (really funny guy). He started to tell me about the history of the stadium and how his whole family had attended the school. I asked him if he had attended and he said, "No." I laughed hysterically because we had just had an entire conversation about all of his family members attending and he did not. I asked him to do a documentary and he was really excited to participate. He gave me a quick rundown on the Percell Stadium as well as the school. *Pause: I would like to take the time to say Rest in Peace to his father Paul Rooney dubbed the 'Golden Boy' who ran the medical center and died of cancer. I really enjoyed talking to that guy and hope that I served him justice by mentioning his father's name in my book. Play:*

Upon leaving the area I decided to treat myself to Ponderosa Steakhouse buffet. I thought that I deserved it since I will not be eating well for awhile once I touch down in Chicago. I put twelve pieces of chicken in a napkin and stuffed it in my pocket for dinner later. I gassed up and hit the road - Chicago bound.

About twelve minutes in, I began to hear noises coming from under the hood. I had to turn down the radio to actually hear the engine because I had just gotten my car fixed. I paid twenty eight hundred dollars to put in a new engine but since it was used I was already leery. I continued to listen to the noise as it got louder. "Please no," I thought to myself as I tried to convince myself that if I continued to drive the noise would eventually go away. I kept saying 'no' as I pulled over to the side of the road. After sitting in my car for half an hour feeling bad I had to remind myself that it was only me in this outside world. There was no one to call. No one to turn to. No one who can help me. I called roadside assistance and gave my location. *Pause: I was really hoping that the problem was only a fuel pump which I could scramble up some money for. Play:* When the tow truck guy came he made me feel better because he told me that the issue was probably only the fuel pump. He was nice enough to drive me to a hotel room which was in walking distance to the shop. I cleaned up my foot and took myself a nice hot shower. All I could think of was the sign that read, "ninety miles to Chicago." I began to think to myself, *I don't care if I hit the city, rode around and then went back to Virginia. I had to at least hit the city.* Then, out of the blue I received an email from a woman by the name of Deborah Jones. It reads:

Well Hello:

> *I am your neighbor across the street from your old house…A.J.'s mom, the one with the huge trash container. I just had to write you after A.J. showed me the article of you in the Voice and just say I admire the awesome journey that you are committed to and wish I had just met and chatted with you before you decided to leave your residence. I love talking to MY people that think outside of the box. You are traveling a road that a lot of us dread to go. They don't know nor do they want to know the how or the why of homelessness, yet it can happen in the wink of and eye. I know…I have worked for over twenty years with DSS on the frontline and was too close for comfort the four years waiting for approval of my SSD. I just have to give you your props and let you know I will be following your journey. I know sometimes it will be rough but just keep on…Peace*

Now for that email to reach me at the very moment of debating homeward or Chicago it almost brought a tear to my eye. It was then that I decided that there was no way in hell I was going to give up. This project was bigger than me…bigger than what little setbacks that I could ever go through. There were people who had been or almost been in the shoes that I was about to put on. I began to feel the excitement of the people who were backing me and it empowered me. Those people are the people that inspire me to pursue my dreams at all cost. I can't worry about a car, sickness, injuries or anything else because what rested upon my shoulders was far greater than the physical pain that the world could dish at me. I had people's hopes, dreams, and prayers resting on me. Even if the elements around me may have begun to break down, those people's hopes and dreams would never be able to take a backseat. For these reasons and these reasons alone I will push forward.

January 2nd

I received a phone call bright and early from the mechanic telling me that the problem was the engine. My feelings were hurt sorely but when things go wrong in my life my brain instantly begins to think of ten other options to correct the situation. I asked the mechanic to pick me up, grabbed as many of my bags as I could and got on a bus heading ninety miles to Chicago. Not having the faintest idea what I was going to do when I got there; I was on my way.

I made two phone calls while on the bus. One was to a female that had hit me up on facebook saying she had family in Chicago and would possibly be able to assist me. The other was to my uncle back in Virginia. My uncle's ex-wife's sister lived in Chicago and even though that was one phone call that I knew he did not want to make he made it. I spoke to Gretchen (my uncle's ex wife) who told me that she would call her sister in Chicago and they would assist me in any way that I needed. She told me to make sure that I handled my business and she was proud of the move that I was making. In less than ten minutes I began to receive phone calls from both of her sisters who were overjoyed to help me. I found out that Gretchen had two sisters in Chicago and that they both were eager to help me. They called me several times to make sure I would have a roof over my head and to continuously give me directions through the city so I could get to a location where they could pick me up.

Getting off of that bus and actually stepping on Chicago ground was pure bliss. I stopped and asked several people for directions and they all appeared very friendly unlike the people in New York. In Chicago, when you ask for directions even if they did not know the directions they would still try to give you some directions. I couldn't even be mad if I got lost a few times because I was in Chicago. I was carrying a total of eight bags which is a very hard task to accomplish. When a female saw my struggle, she walked over to assist me. She grabbed two of my bags and helped me walk to a cab. I was impressed that she helped.

Chicago is a huge city! I took a cab to another train station and struggled to carry those bags inside the terminal. I will tell you one thing...I NEEDED A

DRINK. I felt the need to celebrate. Against all odds I was in Chicago. Carelessly I had a hole in my foot but I had a roof over my head and no longer needed crutches. I stopped in the restaurant in the terminal and purchased a cranberry and vodka. Even though I knew that one task was over I knew that I was back at the starting line all over again. I can deal with that as long as one part was accomplished. Gretchen's oldest sister (Bridget) met me at the train station. She was a very astute woman and I thought we hit it off very well, although; I don't think she approved of me stopping at the store to buy cigarettes, beer and a box of duchess. But, as my Aunt Judy always told me, "You're a Goode…always be yourself." I got the feeling that she was a 'churchy' kind of woman but I didn't really care. I got to her apartment which was on the 14th floor in the rich part of Chicago. I spent my first night at the gym (which was in the building) and ironing my clothes for the next day. *Pause: I took two of my Percocet's and drank two beers. I began to get very dizzy and lightheaded. Please don't mix drugs and alcohol…potential of being a very dangerous combination (hahahahahaha). Play:*

January 3rd

I woke up this morning feeling refreshed and was ready to get it in… *"Chicago here I come!"* I was fully prepared to meet resistance at every corner. I knew that just because I was here or since I was a 'big shot' in Richmond meant absolutely nothing to the people in Chicago. I knew that I wasn't going to show up and be an instant star.

The first place I headed was Harpo studios even though I knew nothing was going to come of it. I just had to see the building and remember what my goal was. Of course the security guard shut me down at the door upon me attempting to enter (and that was cool). I had also forgotten that Oprah was out of the country with her fans celebrating her upcoming birthday. I actually felt a sigh of relief because it meant that I could gather my thoughts and formulate a plan. I saw a couple of free press newspaper stands and grabbed a few papers. I called a few papers (which for future business reasons I will not name) but I was shocked with some of the responses that I received. Most of the papers that I talked to told me that they only did popular trendy issues and that they did not care for an aspiring artist. I was told that if I got my name mentioned by Oprah that they would feature a story on me. *Pause: Well duuuh…if I was to be mentioned by Oprah then I probably wouldn't be calling you and when I actually do make it, I promise to not breathe a word in your direction. Play:* I do understand the newspapers' position and I'm fully ready for a struggle. I know that it will be many no's before I receive a yes. I'm ready for all of those no's but fully expect to receive that yes.

January 4th and 5th

These days I spent brainstorming. I spent my time on the computer emailing different companies, radio talk shows and acquiring tickets to any live audience that I could get to. I enjoyed living on the west side of Chicago in the Pavilion apartment building. I stayed on the 14th floor with an inside and outside pool, restaurant, fitness center, and racquet ball room. The place was truly laced. I think I was starting to get comfortable with my set-up. Just a few days ago I was sleeping in a hospital and now I was living in a penthouse. It reminded me of one of my greatest phrases from the movie Titanic. When the woman asked Leonardo DiCaprio if he liked living the way he was (homeless) he responded, *"Well last night I was sleeping under a bridge and now I'm wining and dining with you fine folks here."* That line still makes me laugh and gives me the inspiration needed to keep moving forward. I believe that what I'm doing is what life is…what I'm doing is living. I fully expect to enjoy every single moment of it. I need people to understand that not knowing what's to come next is truly living. It invokes emotions that need to be invoked. People should know that being afraid, shocked, amazed, excited, happy and sad all comes with living. People always think that I am not afraid of anything but the reality is… I am afraid of everything. It's only when you walk through whatever scares you that you then understand that there was actually nothing to be afraid of. If you spend your entire life knowing each and every little step then you will have led a very boring life.

January 6th

I spent this day getting back to the basics of writing which is the only time I feel completely comfortable with myself. I had already began shooting one of my mini-series and continued to write on that story. I received a call from a blocked number which excited me. *Pause: I was excited because I never know which call will be "the one".* *Play:* It ended up being Bridgette's (the lady I was living with) boyfriend. *Pause: Keep in mind that this joker must be about fifty years old or so.* *Play*: Instantly I felt no love from this phone call. My instincts were right. He instantly came off confrontational and judgmental. I understood his insecurities but his approach made me take a step back and look at the phone. I had to keep in mind that she was keeping a roof over my head for the time being but this dude was putting me in a place that I really was trying to stop myself from going.

He told me that staying at his girlfriend's house was hindering him from spending time with her. He expressed how bad I was in the way and that I did not know if he was paying her bills or not. *Pause: Seriously I didn't give a fuck if he was paying the bills or not. Play:* I controlled my temper and tried to explain to him that the journey I was on was faith based and that in my family when someone needed help we helped. He told me that was wrong and stupid and he represented Chicago and his way was the true blue north way. I knew that he was wrong and some people (mainly people with money) will continue to have the same views and opinions that they proceeded to have no matter how hard I try to get them to see a different viewpoint. It's kind of like republicans and democrats (ha-ha). I found it strange that he would rather see a man homeless than to help him with their dream. Maybe he had issues with being insecure. Either way it was time for me to get off the phone because he really had no idea who I really was. He told me that Bridgette did not even have a problem with me living at the apartment but he had more of an issue with it. He told me that he wanted me out by Saturday which was irritating since he was telling me this on a late Thursday evening. I can bite my tongue and be respectful on the phone but this is my book and I can freely express myself here.

Pause: Dude…that was a punk ass move to call me from a blocked number. It's kind of unfair that you got my number and called me but you had the audacity to block your number. When you say 'man to man' that means that we are both playing on even grounds. Let's just say you may have won the battle but the war is all mine. Now back to the book. My fault...let me say it again...PUNK ASS MOVE. Okay now we're back. Play:

About a half hour after getting off the phone with him Bridgette's younger sister called me fussing about the same thing. They both said they wanted me out by Saturday which was only two days away. I didn't have a problem with any of this but they were acting as though I had committed a heinous act since I had been around. I could handle whatever came my way but what took the cake was when Bridgette came home and asked for the key to the top lock. That was really weird since I had both keys the entire time I had been here but now she was requesting one of the keys back. Of course she did it in a slick way as though I was stupid. *Pause: Reenactment time...Bridgette walked in the room where I was sitting. Apparently she was on the phone with her sister and while on the phone she came towards me stating she needed the top key because her younger sister had lost her spare key. Now, let me know who loses one key off the key ring? Play:* It made me upset that she would think that I would duplicate a key or even attempt to steal from her especially since she was providing a roof over my head. I was upset that they would dare insult my intelligence by attaining the key in this manner. I would have rather she been a woman about it and asked for the key back. I would have respected her a lot more if she had called me a 'would be' thief to my face.

Pause: You must understand that both sisters were inspired by my story when I first told them, but they let their cloudy judgment lose out on my vision. Whether they know it or not I am eternally grateful for them opening their doors to a complete stranger. They were a part of my journey or as I would like to say my movie as I view my life as a movie. They played a great scene in my movie called life but when the scene is over...it's over. I must move to the next portion of the movie. I will say it again...I am grateful for the family for helping me get a start in Chicago. Play:

January 7th

I woke up knowing that I had to find a new place to rest my head. It actually felt good leaving the house on a new mission. I'm a people's person and I need to be around people and see sights. I got off the train and began to walk to find the local YMCA since I heard they had housing. *Pause: I had only heard of YMCA housing in the movies. Around my way the YMCA were only gyms. Play:* The person I talked to on the phone when I called told me that they housed "less fortunate" people. I had a few dollars on me but being homeless meant that I had to choose between cigarettes, eating or even riding a bus. I understood the value of a dollar because once it was gone it was gone. I made the decision to walk, I bummed a cigarette and I decided to go hungry. It didn't matter how bad my physical urges were I had to save what little money I had because I didn't know what the future would entail. I walked for three and a half hours with the hole in my foot beginning to hurt and bleed again. But I had to continue to walk because... hell, what else was I going to do?

I made it to the YMCA and was forced with the embarrassment of telling people that I was homeless and broke. Even though I was "homeless" and low on money; I felt it very degrading to tell people my situation. I never really understood the phrase "in a blink of an eye" until I was put in the situation that I put myself in. I also learned a new phrase "when it rain it pours" because when things start snowballing down it don't stop until it completely boils over. I didn't feel homeless because I was wearing a pea coat and scarf and the people walking in the building look dirty and unkempt. The receptionist showed me and an older white gentleman around the YMCA. He was well dressed in a two piece looking dignified. We both looked as though we were trying to hold on to the last piece of dignity that we had left. While doing the walk through with the receptionist I realized we were no different than the "homeless" looking people we saw walking past us...just had on better clothes. It made me wonder what they wore when they walked in.

The grand tour consisted of the receptionist showing us the shower area, T.V. room, computer room where we could only be on the computer for an hour a day, and our own private room. She was very informative and polite. The room that she showed me was very small. It was no bigger than the size of a dorm room; Small... but much more room than I actually needed. There was a desk, chair and a bed which was all I really needed. The only thing that I cared about was peace and quiet to write and I was happy. Rightfully so, I was unaware that this room costs three hundred and sixty six dollars a month. *Pause: I mean...how could the* "homeless" people that lived there afford to pay for it? Yes...I had the money but didn't want to spend it on a place to live. I didn't know how long I was going to be in the rat race, so I had to be prepared to go the distance. *Play:* After the receptionist realized that I couldn't pay for the room she gave me insight on how social services paid rent for up to three months when the recipient did not have any money or paperwork. She informed me that since I was walking I would never make it to the social services building in time since it was two thirty in the evening. She suggested that I could head to the homeless shelter where I could rest my head and eat for the weekend. I thanked her for the assistance and exited the building.

As soon as I got around the corner I flagged down a taxi because I was determined to make it to the social services building but I didn't want the receptionist to see that I had money to take a taxi. *Pause: Once you mention free to me, I'm on the go! I would have run the whole way there if I thought it was close enough. Play:* The cab ride cost me twenty dollars of money that I didn't have but I told the cabbie to step on it. *Pause: I wonder... why do these cab drivers think that I have to tip them? I have never tipped anyone at McDonalds for their services and I wasn't going to tip them. The driver seemed to have an attitude because he didn't get a tip.*

Play: I made it to the social services building at 2:45pm and was once again met with resistance. The social services people told me that it was too late in the day to be seen. My brain went into overdrive because I refused to waste 20 dollars to get here and leave without utilizing every option that I have. I asked the guy at the reception desk where the bathroom was and snuck into the elevators to the second floor. I walked into the room and sat down quietly. A man walked out of the office and did a double take after seeing me sitting there. I tried to keep my head down and not be noticed but I couldn't ignore him walking to the banister and yell to the first floor, "I thought I told y'all not to send anyone else up." I was super embarrassed (ha-ha). The security guard approached me and told me once again that I could not be seen today. They gave me some papers to fill out and told me that I could stay in the holding area that they had set up for homeless people on the first floor. I took the papers and walked in the bathroom and saw this guy sniffing coke in the stall beside mine. I then walked past the holding area and saw people drinking beer, talking loud and cursing.

Pause: I'm not racist against my own people in the least but I was not about to be the only light skin person in that room either. I was wearing a pea coat...I had an iphone and I am not stupid in the least. I would rather go back to the lady who was trying to put me out instead of stay in that room. You should have seen the look on those people's face when I asked for directions to the rich part of the city. I was fully prepared to be homeless but I wasn't ready to be quite that deep in the mix. Play: Between fight and flight...I jumped hurdles to get away. But I knew eventually I wouldn't have a choice. When I was in the army I really hated getting dirty. When we would go to the field, the first thing my sergeant would do was grab dirt, throw it on himself and rub his hands in it. He told me that if you're going to get dirty it was no use in procrastinating. That stood true for a lot of things in my life and was a very valuable lesson for me. If it's something that has to be done...just do it! If it's inevitable then adjust mentally and dive right in. I knew my time was soon enough.

January 8th

I heard her in the living room cleaning. I had pretty much tried to stay out of her way when she was there. Sitting on that bed looking out the window is when I decided that I should start writing about my path to Oprah. After journaling the beginning days of this journey I went back to sleep and was awaken by the sound of knocking at the door. It was Bridgette telling me that I needed to clean the room (wow I felt like a little kid). She left and sent me a text later saying that she would be having her book club meeting from 3-6:30pm. This of course meant that I shouldn't be there and I bet not show my face for those hours. *Pause: One thing that continues to confuse me is that I am an aspiring author and she is in a book club. This would be the most opportune time to get my name circulated, but that's what I'm talking about when I say cloudy judgment. I try to show people my vision but if they are wearing sunshades then my light will be dim. Play:* I didn't even ask her because I knew what the answer would be.

I knew that one day my book would grace her book club and coffee table. You know what I find funny...when I make it big and people begin to reminisce over me...how much will their stories of me change. *Pause: For the people that don't know, that's Pete Rock and C.L. Smooth's, "When They Reminisce Over You." Listen to it. It's a great song. Play:* I cleaned the room to perfection, showered and left for the day. I needed time to unclog my brain. I can lose focus on my own vision if the elements around me aren't right.

I took the train to Harlem Irving Plaza (H.I.P). I walked in and was sadly disappointed. I saw so many people buying so many things that they did not need. So much money wasted while so many people lay hungry or homeless in the streets and around the world. These were the type of people who would pay three hundred dollars for a sweater or scarf, but wouldn't give a dollar to charity because they "don't have it" or "don't trust where the money is going." It made me think of all the frivolous things that I have personally spent money on. I have thrown away money at bars, clubs, clothes or just plain stupid stuff. I instantly knew that I had to leave the mall.

I tried to locate the closet museum or anything that would cultivate my mind. But by it being so late in the evening everything was too far or it was just too late in the evening for me to venture out to. I found a bookstore that was in walking distance from the mall and I felt more comfortable sitting in that bookstore's café writing than I did when I was surrounded by people at the mall. I spent the day gathering my thoughts and decided that I needed time to just chill and get my thoughts together. I have to make myself slow down sometimes because I move fast and think a lot. I went to the all you can eat Chinese buffet and went to watch a movie. I saw Fighter, a movie about a boxer name Mickey Ward who came from the bottom to the top. I love movies that show triumph.

January 10th

I returned to Social Services and even though I was in the same situation as the people around me it felt as though I shouldn't have been there. Even at that time of struggle I still felt as though there was a light upon me. I felt out of place sitting in that building. I wondered if other people felt like I did on their first visit walking in this building. Like I said before, I understood how people got into this situation but I cannot understand how people become comfortable in their situation. I heard people complaining of the long wait time to see a counselor.

Honestly, I was ashamed and embarrassed to be asking for help. I sat in that building for eight hours before finally speaking to a counselor. After finally speaking to a counselor; I told the counselor that I made twelve dollars an hour in November and did not work in December. He told me that I made too much money in the last two months to receive any benefits. He did offer a spot to stay in the shelter nightly, but I had to leave every morning. Also, he offered me a warm meal and a place to rest my head nightly but I still wasn't ready for that option at the time. I still had a trick in my bag.

My friend had suggested that I stay in a storage unit. He told me that some of the units were climate controlled. *Pause: Hey…as crazy as it sounded it didn't actually seem like a bad idea. Play:* One of the things that I really love about my friends is that they know that I am a little off the rocker but they still support and encourage me in each and every way. They truly want to see me succeed.

I headed towards the facility (I'll leave the name of the company out of the book for the sake of the employees). After speaking to the employee; I was given their special, a unit in the basement which was bigger than the room that I had requested at a cheaper price. I thought to myself, *"hey this could actually work and for only 57 dollars a month."* The order of operation was that the office opened at 9am and the gates stopped opening at 10pm which of course meant that I had to be out of the storage daily by 9am and in nightly by 10pm. That was cool with me because I needed to be on the streets talking to people as much as possible. I taught myself how to work Google maps (which is a hard task since I am computer illiterate) and I was off to the 24 hour gym.

My cousin had suggested that if all else failed that I should at least get a gym membership that way I could move around to different gym locations and sleep. Another friend of mine from Richmond told me that she had a cousin in Chicago who could help me out in that area. That person gave me the hook-up and instead of me paying $250 (the regular gym price) I ended up paying 70 dollars for the entire membership and I could terminate the membership at will.

I had a good stress free workout and made it to the storage unit by 9:30pm. The first night in the storage unit was really scary and cold. I knew there were cameras in the building and if they ever viewed them I would be put out immediately. I thought that climate controlled meant that it would be comfortably warm but I slept on the concrete slab and that chilled my body much more. I also came to an understanding that the outside temperature played a role on the inside temperature of the unit. It was one of those cold nights that made me think, *"What the hell am I doing?"* I pulled out all of my clothes out of my bags and attempted to make a bed on the ground. After laying and freezing on the ground for about 45 minutes I sat up and tried to fall asleep leaning against the wall but that was a metal plate which was colder than the floor. I woke up three times before 3am and saw my phone had gone dead which is a very important tool because I needed to know the time in order to be out. I woke up again thinking that it must be around 5am. I crept out of my quarters and plugged up my phone looking at the time. It read 8am and I thought to myself, *"Wow…I can actually do this…I can actually do this."*

January 11th

I left the storage unit today with pep in my step. I had thought of an angle that I could try out. I knew that my words were inspiring and had power but the problem was getting people to hear them. I came up with the idea to make a billboard that would serve as my 'website' detailing the *Traces of You* project as well as my journey. The idea came out of nowhere which is mainly where most of my ideas come from (ha-ha). I decided that I would stand outside of Harpo studios daily until somebody took notice of me. I knew that the show would be over in three months and that would mark the end of my journey. I knew the cold weather would be a huge hurdle so I had to spend money buying boots, hats and gloves to battle the weather. Everything came up to 15 dollars but that wasn't money I was ready to spend at the current time so I took the price tags off and put everything on acting as though I walked in the store with them on. *Pause: Oh Karma…as Karma would have it; leather gloves do absolutely nothing against the cold weather. Play:* This is another valuable lesson that I was learning on this journey and a habit I was trying to break out of. Stealing is not a good trait no matter how small the stolen object is. If a person does not have then they must do without or simply ask.

I went to the gym and started working on my poster. I found it quite funny that when I was in my own little world working on my project that people wanted to know what I was doing. I noticed people attempted to peer over my shoulder to see what I was writing. A few courageous ones who stopped to talk to me were really impressed by my project. The words of encouragement that I received made me continue to push forward. A lot of times I felt the need to give it all up and head back home. A lot of times my mom was the strength that encouraged me to go forward at all odds. She told me that when I was ready to throw the towel in she would throw it in, as well. I have my own issues with religion but I understand I need to pray to something bigger than me. I continuously need to restore faith in myself letting myself know that everything will be okay. I operate the same way to this day. I knew that this journey would not be easy but I also knew in my heart that out of all people who could make it…I could.

I was excited to get my "billboard" project started. I told people that I would do whatever it took to get on the Oprah show no matter if that meant standing outside in the cold until I got recognized. I am a man of my words and that is exactly what I planned on doing. It was time for me to get back to the storage unit which I started to hate because I didn't like being on a time schedule. On my bus ride back I received a call from my brother which was cool because he is really involved in my project. I say this because he is a great rapper and wanted to be the one who "brought home the gold". We talked for an hour and I felt love that I never felt before. My family continues to be the strength I need to carry forward.

At this moment another idea hit me like a ton of bricks. I thought it was time to broaden my resume and give directing a chance. I chose a story (Margaret) out of my book which would be an easy scene. It was a scene that I knew very well since it took place in Richmond, Va. I knew that Richmond needed a spark of "life" which I believed I could give to them. I chose the church that my grandmother used to attend to use even though they were down to only a few members. The power of my mind amazes me once I had the strength to unlock it. Here I was with no degree, six months previously about to end my own life and now about to direct my own movie. It felt good to hear my mother tell me how proud she felt when people spoke so highly about her son. It didn't matter what happened in my own personal life. No matter how bad the situation I was in seemed, my mother would always raise her head up high. That far exceeded my thoughts of giving up. Forget the fact that I was living in a storage unit. Forget the fact that I slept on a cold floor nightly. My mom was proud and it was me that was giving her that pride. I couldn't and wouldn't quit.

On a different note, I bought an air mattress from Marshall's because I refused to sleep another night on that hard floor in the storage unit. The air mattress package came with an air pump but no batteries. I was not about to spend more money on batteries so I used the air in my lungs (that's right). Smoking and exhaling all that air is a very tiring ordeal. It took me over an hour to fill that queen size mattress up and I had to stop several times to catch my breath, but I managed to fill it up all the way. I set that mattress on the ground and lay on top of it for a few minutes. That was one of the best days of my entire trip. That was the last thoughts that went through my head as I fell asleep.

January 12th

I spent the majority of the day putting the finishing touches on my poster. I also had to make my way to the "lady" house so I could retrieve the rest of my belongings. On my way, I received a phone call from the Chicago Reader, a local newspaper. *Pause: Now that put a smile on my face. Play:* The reporter asked me a bunch of thorough questions and my answers intrigued him. He told me that he wanted to run it pass his editor to see what he thought of the story. The editor thought it was great and loved the concept of my journey. That was more motivation for me. I mean that gave me a great boost. I told the lady about my impromptu interview and she seemed very taken back. "Wow that was quick," she said. I know that people don't understand that I am in Chicago for a purpose. I didn't care about meeting females, clubbing or working for someone else. My purpose and my sole purpose is Oprah. Now don't get it twisted the females are very lovely and even though I was tempted a lot I knew that just one female would throw things out of whack. I had to stay positive and focused. Plus who wants to talk to the person who is homeless and has no money to spend.

January 13th

This was the day I would do my trial run. I got a hearty lunch from Panera bread, which I must say makes the best grilled cheese sandwich that I have ever eaten. I took the bus to 1058 West Washington Street, home of Oprah Winfrey's studio. I chose a spot across the street from the garage because I knew people would see me as they drove in and out. I set up my poster and imagined myself walking through those doors one day. A few employees came outside to smoke and I approached them and asked them to read my poster. On one hand, I was turned down numerous of times and couldn't believe that people would actually turn me down on simply reading a poster. On the other hand, I understood that they were working and a smoke break was all that they had to get away from the craziness.

This is when I began to learn another lesson…Patience. One thing that I learned about myself is that when I rush into a situation nothing works out because I move too fast. However, when I relax and let things come to me then things would be just fine. I had come way too far to give up because things didn't work out in a few days. I saw a brother walk out and called him over to read my poster. He skimmed over the poster and focused on the word homeless, took a look at me and labeled me. He instantly lost my vision and labeled me. He judged a book by its cover which is what a lot of people tend to do when they meet people. Instantly his arrogance turned into an "I'm better than you" state. This is the kind of attitude that I fight ferociously.

He told me that I would never make it into Harpo studios with the route that I was on. *Pause: He had no idea the kind of person that he was dealing with. Play:* On his behalf, he told me that he worked at a mission that assisted homeless people and offered to provide me with a meal. I told him that he lost the point of stand that I was making. I guess he got the message and kindly excused himself. He got into his car and pulled off. I wanted to give it one more attempt and give him an audio c.d. book that he could listen to. As he sped past he raised his hand and refused to look in my direction. A few minutes later I spoke to the maintenance who told me that he has never seen a person make it in the doors holding a sign but wished me the best. I was cool with each rejection.

Perseverance - steady persistence in a course of action… A purpose in spite of difficulties, obstacles or discouragement. Don't worry…I knew I wasn't going to be an overnight success story, but I will be a success story against all odds.

Even though they both provided discouraging words, I wasn't going to give up. I left after the cold of Chicago swept through my entire body for four hours. I could literally feel hypothermia setting in my body. My fingers started to become numb and began to curl up in a ball by the minute. I tried to stretch out my hand and could not. I power walked to the closet Starbucks and quickly ducked into the restroom. I had to put my hands in my pants between my legs to warm them up. I remembered that body heat was the best way to warm up and to not submerge my hands in hot water for the fear of shock. *Pause: Yea I kind of paid attention in some of those first aid classes I attended. Play:* After talking to my mother and a few friends I spent some time writing which is the only thing that snaps me back to reality. A pad and a pen is all I need to escape the harsh realities of the outside world.

January 14th

Wooooow…two weeks in the game and I'm still here. Good stuff. I woke up this morning with a new feeling. Today I could better prepare myself for the cold of the world. My friend had given me some feet warmers. *Pause: You put those little packets in your shoe or glove and the crystals warm you up…go figure. Play:* I put on three pairs of socks and two shirts along with a fleece to be layered up. I grabbed my sign and back to Harpo studios I went. Now, I was finally mentally and physically prepared. I had overcome the fear of looking crazy standing outside of Harpo studios and felt comfortable. I set up my sign and put my headphones on allowing my mind to drift. I didn't allow myself to focus on the future I only focused on enjoying the moment right then and there.

I observed the scene and noticed the employees walking to the Starbucks around the corner. The plan I formulated is that I would stand outside Harpo studios for an hour and warm up in Starbucks for twenty minutes. This way I could control the possible onset of hypothermia. A couple of times I had to force myself to take that break because once my brain started zoning I hated breaking that moment. I knew that standing out here for three months would take a toll on my body, so I was forced to pace myself. The first time I walked back from my break a white man pulled over, wished me good luck and gave me an apple. After my second break an electrician came over and asked me about my poster. He told me that he had seen me the previous day and wanted to read my poster. He gave me positive feedback which is the actions I needed to continue to carry on. Those two people showed me that people were watching even when I didn't know that they were.

Then, the security guard from the apartment building I stood in front of came out and told me that someone had complained about me standing in front of the building and threatened to call the cops. I asked him, "What could the police do?" He replied, "Nothing," so I told him to let her call the cops. As long as I was in the right what could the police really do? Oh but then I remembered that I had weed in my bag. *Pause: Yea...I bet you weren't ready for that one...ha-ha. Play:* Since I've always had a problem with authority I didn't want to risk talking to them. My attitude can become somewhat of a problem when I know that I'm in the right. Since I knew that I was 'dirty' I knew this wasn't going to be a good look. Defeated, I decided to call a quits for the day. I felt like the day had gone well though.

I went back to the Starbucks one last time to warm up before heading to the gym. As I sat there I saw this woman giving a guy an interview. I was drawn to her because of the way she used her hands while she talked. Later, I found myself starring at her. I had to say something to her. When she finished interviewing, I asked her what she did and she told me that she was a director. *Pause: Wooow...the odds of that. It's so weird how things work out for me. Situations like this always work out for me. If the woman in that apartment building had not complained about me standing in front of it I never would have gone inside Starbucks at that very moment and met a director. Weird....but these types of things have happened to me my entire life. Play:* I showed her my poster and we got in a nice conversation about my journey, trials and tribulations. I like the fact that I as a person had intrigued her and not the book...not yet. I gave her one of my audio c.d. books and she said that she did not know how to help but would keep me in her prayers.

Since I got off of work early (ha-ha) I headed to the gym in a relaxed state of mind. I played a great game of basketball and got a free protein shake (no I did not steal it). Then, I called a few of my friends to invite them to my mini movie I was planning to shoot in Richmond, VA on February 5th (which I was becoming real excited about) and got great responses. I was in a great mood. It was one of those days that I didn't want to end at 10pm. *Storage rules you know.* But, I ended today sitting on the floor writing to you about my journey...Ice Cube said, "Today was a Good Day."

January 15th

Saturday...wooow...I woke up and thought to myself two weeks and a day. I moved to Chicago not knowing anyone or knowing where I was going to stay and I am still here. I have a roof over my head (self storage unit) and a regular schedule. I think I'm proud of my progress so far. I still have a long way to go but so far it's kind of cool. Another lesson that I've learned is that I must take little breaks from this stressful life and enjoy things by myself. Taking breaks gives me a chance to gather my thoughts and move forward with whatever project that I'm working on. I went to the movie theatre which gave me a break from the world of facebook, my family and friends, and Oprah. Just took a chance to relax. While I was in a relaxing mode *(which is when great thoughts hit me)* it dawned on me that maybe people were avoiding me because I looked homeless. The clothes I wore and my hair uncut were all reasons for people to look at me differently. I knew how I saw myself *(it didn't matter what I wore but rather the intelligence level)* but the world was still superficial and at times will judge a book by its cover before ever reading it.

My poster is my resume but my appearance has to match the job that I am searching for. So, I decided that I would get my haircut and iron some of my clothes, even though it was below freezing temperatures, I was going for the job of my life. I couldn't worry about any mental stress or how the cold weather would take a toll on my body because I knew that back in Richmond my mother's friends were talking to her about me and she was holding her head up high. *Pause: I feel like my entire family has someone to look up to. It's been a long time since someone in this family has sparked that kind of energy. My grandma who saw so much pain and strife in her life proved to be my biggest motivator. She is the rock of the entire family. I sometimes feel like when she dies the strong family unit that we have will somehow die without her. This family has never had money but we've always had a tremendous amount of love. We are always together on Sundays no matter what the issues are and I couldn't let that die. It is up to me to keep the family together and for that purpose I will risk hyperthermia, cold lonely nights in storage units, and I will eat chicken sandwiches no matter if it has been sitting for two days at a time. My family support supports me.*

Play: People ask me all the time why I choose Oprah. For one, it doesn't matter how graphic the stories in *Traces of You* are there is always a love ending….to me that's an Oprah crowd. Two, about a year and a half ago mentally I was going through a rough patch in my life and the only way I knew how to break free was to kill myself. If you don't know by now how my brain works I'm a very literal person. I could visualize myself putting the knife to my veins and blood leaking down my arm. I imagined me tying some of my bed sheets together, wrapping them around the banister and jumping with my neck snapping and my body swinging back and forth against the wall. But the plan I thought of was to write a letter to each person who ever meant something to me and send each one to Oprah and at the end of each letter I would state that I was putting another bullet in the chamber. At the end of all the letters that I had written I was going to pull the trigger and end it all. After I had written about six letters (*each one being over nine pages long*) I realized I had so many more letters to write. I thought to myself, *"Why the hell am I going to kill myself? There are way too many people that love me."*

Figuratively speaking, I had already placed myself in the grave and when the casket was closing I put my hands up and stopped it. When I jumped out of that casket…my feet touched the ground and I decided that it was not time yet. That experience made me see the world in a whole new and different light. I smelled fragrances that I had never smelled before. I fell in love with the architecture of the buildings that I was used to seeing but never noticed. I saw that people were truly beautiful on the inside no matter how ugly their outside appearances were. I understood that generally people wanted more out of life but didn't know how to achieve it. I understood that people wanted to help people even if they didn't know how. I found out that the first step in getting help is to ask for it. People wanted to help but didn't know how sometimes. I know how to help people and I am determined to do just that.

January 16th

Today was an offset day. I started off in pretty good spirits. I went to the gym to get a quick workout in and I was going to try and meet the "Lady" today to retrieve the rest of my belongings from her house. I was down to my last two hundred dollar check and went to four check cashing stores to cash it and found out that they did not cash personal checks. This taught me another lesson…Don't procrastinate. The day prior I could have went to a bank and handled this but I was too lazy *(puckered out from the gym)* to make it to the bank in time. I did manage to watch some football games at the gym *(probably the same place my team the redskins are watching the game from)*.

After a full day it was time to head home (storage unit) early because I was super tired. Aaaaarrrrgghh…I sat on my mattress and heard the air seething out. Somehow I had wiggled the mattress onto a nail sticking out of the wall. My watched read 8:46pm and there was no time to make it to the store to buy another mattress *(really no money)*. Plus, the storage unit gates stopped opening at 10pm and the bus ride would have taken too long to get back on time. I walked to the local convenient store and bought some gray electric tape. That turned out to be a really good idea until I sat my 230 pound self down on the mattress and the tape popped off. I had spent an hour blowing up the mattress for nothing. I couldn't help but laugh but you know me instantly my brain switched to what I had to do next. I like challenges like this because it makes me think of how I can fix them. I pulled out all the clothes that I had and made a bed on the ground or a pallet as my dad would call it. Of course the clothes were lumpy but it did the trick.

The next day would be Martin Luther King Jr. birthday. My dad *(who is a workaholic)* said that he never worked on MLK day or New Year's Day. I think that's a good rule of thumb to follow. So, I used the internet on my phone to look for events in the area to attend. One thing that I couldn't lose out on was being myself. Even while homeless I have to continue to grow and show respect and homage to the people who made my journey remotely possible. ***To the kids***: *you must continue to grow at all costs which include reading, studying, learning, and cultivating yourself. These are the essential tools needed to lead you out of the mindset that you are in.* Rest in Peace Martin Luther King Jr. Your dream lives on.

January 17th

The day set out to be a really good day because I woke up in a fresh state of mind. Today is Martin Luther King Jr. day and I found an event to attend in his honor. I received a phone call from a good friend of mine who was greatly concerned of the blizzard that was about to blow through Chicago. She wanted me home instead of fighting the snow and she even offered to pay for my ticket. For me this meant two weeks at home and I felt like I wasn't staying true to my game if I left early but her steady persistence held. I told her to book the ticket.

I called Mitch Malone and Community Clovia (radio personalities) in Richmond in an attempt to be on their radio show. I was excited to be coming home but I had to stay productive. I spoke to Community Clovia who told me she was interested but I had to call back because of her busy schedule.

After my quick workout I headed to Northwestern Law School for their MLK celebration. I walked in and saw a table full of food. I was excited about being there but the food put me on cloud nine. *(I was really hungry...ha-ha).* Yea, I ended up getting two plates. I almost felt bad when I walked out of the middle of the ceremony in order to get another plate...*almost felt bad.* Eboo Patel was the speaker who ended up being very good. When a speaker really impresses me I am forced to tell them. I waited in line for him to complete his meet and greet section and overheard a student tell a lady that she had heard her on the radio station that very morning. My ears perked up and I knew I had to meet her as well. Mrs. Aubrey-Wilson was her name and she told me that she thought I was very ambitious...*I liked that.* I worked the system and trailed her until she completed talking to her colleagues and asked if I could assist her with the cleaning process. She gave me her business card and told me to email her.

To the kids*: No matter how scared you are you must take initiative by taking the first step. If you don't know what to say start with 'hello' and after that go with the flow. Remember that you are supposed to be scared. That is part of the process. I feel fear every time I open my mouth to someone new, but you have to conquer those fears. Once you conquer that fear you will understand that you weren't truly afraid at all. In a sense you will feel empowered and will analyze the mistakes that you made. But you will never realize those mistakes until you make the first one.*

January 18th

Today was a slow day. I did the usual and stood outside Harpo studios as I promised with a few perks. I asked this white guy, who had stepped outside to smoke a cigarette, for a cigarette and he asked me about my project. I didn't know what his position was inside the studio but it felt good to tell someone my project. Who knows maybe he can circulate what I'm doing to someone inside. I also got a big boost of energy. I had noticed that usually when people drove up they would have to wait at the garage until it opened but this time I saw the garage open and two security guards walked out and stood at the entrance. About a minute later a black Escalade truck with tinted windows and secret service looking personnel drive right in. I thought that this was very interesting. I don't know who was inside but they must have been very important. That gave me a spark because I know that whoever was in there saw me and I saw them. Like I said before, persistence is the key. I'm betting on people seeing me enough that someone will eventually have to talk to me. Persistence is the key. After the Escalade left…I left.

January 19th

I usually wait until the end of the day to write, but I couldn't pass up this embarrassing morning. Last night I bought some chocolate fiber bars as a snack. Someone should definitely tell people that fiber cleanses your system either that or I'm the dumb one. I ate two fiber bars the previous night and I must tell you *THEY REALLY CLEAN OUT YOUR SYSTEM*. I usually go to Panera bread in the morning to handle my bathroom duties but I was not going to make it and I knew it. I found a Target bag and used a sock to…well you get the point. *Yea yea yea…I know it's disgusting but I had to do what I had to do (ha-ha).*

I would also like to take the time to apologize to a person who is helping me out on my journey. Carey Goodman is a connection that I made back in V.A. who is helping me a great deal on the production of my second movie. When I want something I can be a very aggressive person as well as a little insensitive. So my prayers are with you regarding the death in your family and I hope your mother has a speedy recovery. I truly do thank you for the assistance that you're providing me on this project.

There is a lot of movement going on today at Harpo studios which must mean that they are back to filming again. I knew that the show went overseas for her birthday, but I guess they are back. There were oodles of people standing in line and going in and out of the studios. I stood proudly with my sign knowing that people were noticing me. I know that they think I'm weird but I don't really care. The security guard from the apartment building came out and told me that people were complaining again. This time he gave me a scenario that potential buyers might be deterred from moving in because of my presence. *Pause: Was I (one person) really bringing down the value of an apartment building? Did my presence really not want people to move in? Play:* I was mad at first but after thinking it over it made me realize that people were watching even when I didn't think that they were. I stayed a little longer but I couldn't take the cold anymore and decided to call it a day.

I needed a break from life and decided to go to the movie theatre. I bought three sandwiches from Burger King, put them in my bag and went to the movies. I paid for one but stayed for three: Green Hornet, The Dilemma and True Grit. I just needed a day to relax. While I was watching the movie I got a text from Sam Worley of the local newspaper, Chicago Reader, stating that he would like to meet with me in the morning at 9:30. That gave me a boost of life. Since I'm the one on this journey I begin to feel doubtful at times so whenever I get some good news it would always perk up my senses. That bit of news made me feel like a renewed man. I left to go get a haircut because I knew that I had to look right for this interview. I went to the barbershop, Faith in God. Very fitting name I thought.

I struck up a conversation with the barbers and they allowed me to play one of my tracks from my audio c.d. book (Neverett) for them. They seemed very excited about my project and sent me to WYTEC (Westside youth Technical Entrepreneur Center) which was a very nice youth center. Being a former counselor I was really impressed by their operations. I was instantly greeted at the door by one of the kids who was very courteous and instantly offered me a piece of chicken. *(I turned him down…I know what you're thinking).* The program made me reminisce back to my jobs of youth counseling in Virginia. I talked to an older gentleman who was very knowledgeable which was evident by our conversation on the black movement. He was very impressed by my project and the journey that I was on. He took pictures of me, my board and made a copy of my newspaper clipping. He gave me the general answer that I always receive that he thought that I was heading in the right direction but he did not know how he could assist. He did suggest that I look up Illinois' senator, Ricky Henton, who is very big on young writers and connecting with the community. If I knew that I could get a senator behind me that would be a really big power move. I was told that he had weekly meetings down the street from their building and that would be the best way to contact him. When I left WYTEC I saw a church billboard with a picture of Bishop Fitzgerald. A light came on in my head that I should start talking to local churches and community centers in an attempt to get a reference letter to add to my resume. ***To the Kids:*** *Use your surroundings. If you observe the signs and posters around you, you will notice that they are there to help you.*

January 20th

I stood on my original post outside the Oprah show with my sign. Sam (from Chicago Reader) had asked me how would he be able to pick me out and I told him that I would be the only black guy out there with a sign. Of course he laughed. It was especially cold today but I couldn't take my usual break because I wanted to make sure that he saw me when he walked up. *Pause: Chicago has that kind of cold that chills you to the bone. I could never figure out which direction the wind blew. Play:* Sam walked up looking super cold. He was so cold his nose was turning red. I suggested that we go to Starbucks around the corner which he happily agreed. I really hadn't had a lot of human interaction since I had been in

Chicago so when we started talking it seemed like a flood gate had opened. He took pictures of me and my billboard and asked me to explain what each one of my definitions meant.

Two of my four definitions really stand out to me; Perseverance and Individuality. Perseverance means to continue on with your mission regardless of setback or discouragement. I have had a lot of setbacks, as well as, discouragement from folks who said I was either stupid or crazy. I actually like it when they call me crazy because that just mean that I think differently than them. Individuality is a big one for me. If a person is not free to exercise themselves then that is a form of mental slavery. Example: a person may walk and talk a certain way at home and be comfortable with themselves but as soon as the world begins to critique that person, they will change their actions to benefit others. People have to learn to be comfortable with themselves in spite of society.

The reporter seemed very interested in learning what makes me tick instead of the book. It's always nice when people want to talk about me instead of the book. I like to talk about the book but I like it when people are intrigued by me being me. We talked for close to an hour and an half...so long that he used the bathroom twice and had to flip the tape over to continue the interview. Plus I liked the fact that he had done his research on me before coming to the meeting. I had pulled out my newspaper to show him and he told me that he had already seen them online. This made me feel like he was a pretty thorough guy.

My friend once told me that I should look back on the accomplishments that I've accomplished in the past year. You have to understand that I can't see the things that people see when they talk about me or tell me how great I am. I simply can't see what they see. Once I completely finish one project it feels as though I'm right back at the starting line. Every new project or idea I hit super hard because I fear that I won't get another chance at it again. One of the main things that keep me going is I truly believe that somewhere there is a child watching my Youtube videos saying *"If Goode can make it, I can make it."* This is the honest truth. I am an ordinary person who believes in dreams and dreaming. If dreams are supposed to take you to your wildest imagination then that is where I'm heading and where I want to live at...my wildest imagination. I went back to Harpo studios feeling a little warmer on the inside until Jack Frost slapped me in the face letting me know that he was still around (ha-ha). I called it a day feeling pretty good about myself.

January 21st

I went to Harpo studios but my energy was depleted. I can't force myself to do things because they will turn out poorly. That even stands for my writing. Once my brain says stop I have to stop or else I won't be able to perform to my best ability. So I thought to myself that I should now look into self publishing. By now I have a pretty good following of 1000 people and it would be a good time to get my book on the market. So I found the closet Barnes & Noble's which happened to be on the campus of DePaul. I found a lot of books on self publishing and began to put things in motion. Every book pointed in the direction that I needed to start a website. I called a friend in Richmond who told me that he would help me and give me a free trial offer. You see there's that word again F-R-E-E...that was all I could afford anyway. I also called around and talked to a few people who would help me with the cover to my book. It was time to start giving birth to *Traces of You*. I left the store and found a nice spot on the floor in the common area of the mall where I could write and not be disturbed. I wrote so long that I fell asleep. It wasn't one of those homeless people sleeps but more like *"this dude is working hard"* kind of sleep. When I woke up I saw this female looking at me so I waved her over. In the midst of our conversation she told me that her godfather was in a play the next night and asked me if I wanted to tag along. I gave her my business card and told her that I would be looking forward to her call. It's funny how things are shown even when you are not looking for them to show. It was getting late so I went back to my shack looking forward to the next day.

January 31st

I came home to shoot my second movie. Since I been home it has been a tumultuous trip. It seems as though nothing is working out with my vision but still I have to continue. I understand that this road won't be easy but still I walk. At times I question if the road that I am taking is stupid...but that is only for a brief moment because I truly believe that the road that I am on is intentional. My leaving my job was meant to happen. I understand that everything is meant to happen for a reason.

Another sad thing that I see while being at home is that no one has good news when I talk to them. People complain about the problems that they have and can't seem to figure out the solution. When I'm in Chicago alone I don't think about other people's problems. I only have time to focus on myself. A lot of people focus on the problems that they have at hand and simply put band-aids on the problem instead of focusing on a permanent fix. Nothing stays the same forever but the willpower to endure the problem till the end is the true miracle. I understand that me being back in Richmond solves a lot of other people's problems (because I am very helpful) but they have to understand that they are the question and the answer. I tell people that usually a problem can be solved when they ask themselves the question. I offer a pad and pen and tell them to hold a conversation with themselves. Example: when a woman has been physically abused for the first time her emotions are running rampant. The first emotion is shock followed by the thought of leaving the bastard, immediately followed by the instinct to kill the "muthafucker." But these instincts are washed away with a simple apology that it will never happen again and usually a gift of some sort. All while the woman is thinking "What should I do?" This is an exercise that I truly believe that everyone can learn from.

Beside that...*Traces of You* is slowly progressing. But I believe that as long as I write and keep my head straight it's going to work out. This road to Oprah is the trip that I chose to embark on and I won't look back. The kids are my inspiration and it doesn't matter how many times my mind goes back and forth I will never feel as though the choices that I have made are in vain. It hurts when people don't see my vision. It's hard knowing that I'm special and trying to convince the rest of the world as well...but I will or die trying.

Chapter 3

I know that the fire is hot and even though I fear getting burned my feet continues to walk through it.

February

February 1st

It feels as though I'm idle at home but today is going to be a better day. I'm tired of talking about the book and ready for the birth of *Traces of You*. I talked to a self publishing company today. My biggest fear is that people will try to jerk me around but if they knew the type of person that I am then I'm sure they would think twice. I spoke to Community Clovia again who told me that they don't put people on their show who do not have a website. At times things like this make me upset because I hear rappers who discredit their own race, community and themselves on the radio daily. Every time I turn on the radio I hear songs about sex, killing, drugs, and profanity but nothing to uplift the community. When someone like myself who is positive and outspoken tries to get on the radio there's a struggle. I'm pretty sure if I called females' bitches and hoes I would have a better chance *(yea I'm pretty upset)*. Something else I learned is to take what people say as a learning tool which will in due time sharpen and make me more professional. I can deal with the world that tells me that I'm not professionally ready but woe to the world when I am and they try to turn me down.

February 2nd

Today is the first day that I've felt as though I have been truly productive. I had a great conversation with Kingdom Regal publishing company and I began to work on my website. When I first got home everything was dragging which took a toll on me mentally. I am the type of person who has to stay busy at all times. Being idle tends to lead to destruction for me. I start drinking, partying, and chasing women which is not that bad but I need to stay focused at all times. ***Lesson to the Kids:*** *When conducting business one should always wear appropriate attire. It changes your outlook as well as the way you respond to the questions being asked. If you are in relaxed clothing then the conversation will have more of a relaxed precedent versus wearing business attire which will give you more of a business tone.*

I am really excited to begin the process of getting my book published. People are ready to see a finished copy and in a way…so am I. I know that publishing a book opens my life to criticism which I can handle but I always wonder if my product is good enough for people to enjoy. I just pray that as long as I enjoy what I'm doing then someone else will as well. At the least I just hope the kids who are following me truly see my struggle.

February 3rd

I woke up today pretty excited because I knew that I would get a chance to talk to the church where I would want to shoot my movie. After meeting with the pastor he put a lot of things into perspective. I guess I'm naïve at a lot of things. In my head I assume that when a person has a good idea people are instantly ready to jump for the occasion to help. But just like everything else the church is a business. I understood what the pastor was saying and the position he had to take but when your answer is 'no' then your reasons become identical with everyone else's when they say 'no'. I believe that the church is a place that you can go to when you need help not just spiritual but physical as well. Time after time I am disappointed by how a lot of churches are run.

Allow me to reminisce…there was a time when my sister was down on her luck (no electricity) and she has three kids living with her. I strongly urged her to ask her church (New Birth) for assistance. She told me upon asking for help that she was turned down. That didn't agree with me so well so I took it upon myself to call the pastor personally. After reasoning with the pastor he politely told me that he simply could not take up an offering for a member of the church because the church needed the money for bills. I proceeded to tell him that he can't judge what's in a person's heart and if she only received ten dollars from the offering then that's ten dollars that she did not have at first. *Pause: My family calls me crazy for calling out a pastor like that but hey I feel if you're wrong then you're wrong. Play:* He continued to tell me no which further disappointed my faith in the church.

Sorry…didn't mean to deviate away from the story. The pastor of the church where I was attempting to shoot my movie told me that he would at least ask the members of the choir before he gave me an answer. I could deal with that answer rather than a straight 'no'. I began working on editing (polishing) my book before I sent it off. It is truly a blessing that the publishing company dropped the price of the book from $750 to $550 because they truly understood the plight that I am taking. I know that I am going to encounter many trials and tribulations on this road but I am ready to conquer all that is in my path. I am still on my road to Oprah despite the setbacks, difficulties, obstacles or whatever else may come my way. You hear me Oprah…I'm coming to join you honey…with a *Traces of You* book in my hand. (I say this to you in my best Fred Sanford voice).

February 9th

It's been slow progress but progress nevertheless. I am finally learning how to build my website which seemed like mission impossible at first. I get truly upset when I know that other people in this world know how to do something and I don't. I went out to buy all types of books on website building and called a tremendous amount of people to help me but the learning process all began with me sitting in front of the computer. It took me an hour and a half to figure out how to change the font. It took three hours to figure out how to upload one picture but you know what…I learned how to upload that picture and I figured out how to change the font.

I know that nothing comes at great ease. When I look at a challenge; in the beginning it seems like an impossible task but after completion there is a sense of relief. I always doubt myself with a lot of things that I do but I continuously walk through my challenges. It's like I know that the fire is hot and even though I fear getting burned my feet continues to walk through it. In my lifetime there have always been people who tell me that I have a destiny that I'm destined for. I am always told that I am running from something but I tell them that no one runs from something but they only run towards something. My biggest fear was putting on the shoes to even begin the race. But now that I've started I get to see the people who are cheering me on. Just to think that last year I would have ended my life and would not have been on the road that I am currently on.

Lesson to the Kids: *you must never give up. All the cliché quotes that you hear such as, "if you believe you can achieve," "don't be a fool, stay in school," "nothing beats a failure but a try" these phrases hold power. Think of what you see in your role model…analyze what they posses that you admire, fill those shoes* *and become better. For that role model to become a role model it takes a lot of dedication but it also took a lot of suffering. "With great sacrifice comes great success." The question that I have for you is, "What are you willing to give up to gain success?"*

I have lost a lot of friends, jobs, girlfriends, etc. to follow my heart. My friend asked me if I regret giving up my two jobs and house in order to pursue this path. I quickly replied, "HELL NO" (ha-ha). The path I walk is a lot more fun than the traditional one that everyone else choose to walk on. I am proud of the steps that I am taking.

February 10th

Today production begins. I got the rough draft copy of my book in the hands from Kingdom Regal Publishing. They confirmed that they would bring the price down which as I said before is a true blessing. They are really enthusiastic about the journey that I am on and told me that my book would probably be picked up from a major publishing company and be a best seller. I know they probably tell everyone that but it feels good to hear it being said. Like I said before this process teaches me patience but now I need a finished product so I can begin hustling. My plan is to travel to every city, state, town and set up my stand selling my book. Once again I am afraid of leaving my comfortable boundaries but this is living…this is life.

I continue to have a consistent flow of followers. I found a great artist who sees my vision and is ready to test his limits to make my cover. I love it when someone sees my vision. I spoke to him for an hour and he told me that I was on the right path. I call that encouragement which is much needed. Even though I plan to walk the path that is intended for me I love it when someone encourages me to continue. I feel as I am doing things that people only dream of. People will tell you that the American dream is college, marriage, dog and a big house with the white picket fence, but when does the dream that you once had as a child come into play? Where is the passion that you once had? I feel as though this is the reason why people have mid-life crises; because they look back on their lives and wonder where did all that time go and what have they done for themselves. People live the first eighteen years of their lives committed to school, 4-8 years committed to college and then the rest of their lives committed to another human being.

One time my mother told me that she woke up one day and all of a sudden she felt every bit of 53 years old. She said that she felt as though she had dedicated her entire life to the people around her and felt as though she did not give any part to herself. That's how many people feel as they get older. I personally can't and won't let that happen to me. I can't see myself waking up daily to working and coming home just to start my day all over again. They call me crazy but I see something more than what people call the "good life." I see living as an experience. If I was to die right now I would be excited to see what people would say at my funeral. This is only the beginning of my life and it feels great to see how it will all unfold.

I mentioned this quote before but it is truly my favorite phrase spoken by Leonardo Dicaprio's character in the movie, *Titanic*. It was the scene where the woman asked him if he liked living the way he did and he responded by saying, "Yesterday I was sleeping under a bridge and today I'm wining and dining with you fine folks here." As long as I have a pad and pen and good air in my lungs I'm living life just fine. That's how I envision life. Not knowing where the next steps of life will take me but going in that direction in full force. My friend told me that the life that I'm living is what professor's write their thesis on...get your pens ready because I have a life that will amaze you.

February 18th

Life is good especially when I feel that I'm on the right track. I am working on the website, which I must say that I'm proudly learning on my own. I'm getting the book cover idea together and still posting my Youtube videos. Progress is not bad at all if I must say so. I will say that being at home (V.A.) is not good for my writing. It feels good to be home but so many people demand things that that I don't get a chance to focus on myself. I now have responsibilities; between taking care of my nieces and nephews, chilling with this friend one night and another the next night can be very stressful. My friends think that if I don't get up with them then I'm a fucked up guy. I'm just trying to stay focused. One of my sayings on my poster board is to "refocus but keep the vision the same." I am refocusing and regrouping. *Traces of You* is almost complete and I will have a product to show.

I'm starting to call different churches, lounges, etc. so I can start selling my own product. I will travel city to city and state to state hustling. Once again I have the onset of fear but excitement as well. Once again I will be on my own and traveling. I can't think of a better way to live.

February 20th

Oohhhhh yea...we're getting close to March 4th. My book is about to drop. It's time to get to work. After the feeling that everything was moving slow...*Traces of You* is about to be born. Now is the time to start rejoicing. I will finally have a product to show. I promised all the people that I interviewed that their stories would be published and the day is almost upon us. Yea....let me enjoy this moment. It's not too many times I get to bask in the glory but it sure does feel good. Everyone in my family wants to be in the game and I have something to show in black and white. I see the world and I'm ready to fly. My time to shine...my time to show the world that Raymond Goode can and will.

I'm starting my journey in my own home state first. I will hit every barbershop, beauty salon, church, lounge, bar, club that I can think of to put *Traces of You* in every hand imaginable. I refocused my mind and I'm still heading straightforward to Oprah. I am getting so much help with the website and should be completed by next week. My aunt Judy has played a major role in the building of the website. She and a good friend of mine took me around town to take all of the much needed pictures for the website and other promotional ideas.

I came up with the cover of my own book. It was killing me for the last six months on what it would be. I got ideas and suggestions from everyone, but once I got my brain to relax it hit me in a flash...a total of six minutes.

If you're reading this book I'm pretty sure you read *Traces of You* but if you didn't I will explain the meaning of the cover. The heart has two meanings. One is I wanted it to serve as a ring-holder display that you would see in a jewelry store. The heart also represents the love in the world which is much needed universally.

The rings I thought would be eye catchy. Most females like looking at different engagement and marriage rings so I knew a large crowd of women would be drawn to the cover of the book and pick it up. What stomped me for a minute was the diversity part. Later, it came to me that I would have different nationalities holding the heart from underneath. What I thought was real cool was my Aunt's plan. We went into Walgreen, met random people and asked them to stick their arms under the chocolate box. One of the gentlemen I asked had on a suit which wasn't really in my vision but damn if it didn't put a smile on my face. His suit jacket added finesse to the cover.

My friend told me that I was losing momentum since I hadn't posted any videos on Youtube in a while…homeboy…this is just the calm before the storm. *Traces of you* is hand picked. I picked every portion of my book. I read that most authors should only expect for self-published books to only sell two hundred units in their lifetime. Call me crazy, but I plan on selling that in my first two weeks. *(Lucky I didn't say the first week).* Swag is on 1000 right now.

On another note, I think my mom was a little hurt that I didn't single her out in my "Thank You" section in *Traces of You*. She doesn't know that this book is completely dedicated to her. I showed honor to my grandmother first; who I think is truly deserving of a dedication for the contributions that she's made to this entire family. My mom is the one I get my strength from. I have seen her grow as she has seen me grow. There is no stronger connection that any person can have like I have with my mother. She has stood behind me with every numbskull thing I've ever attempted. She never criticized me but only offered advice along my path. No matter how harsh her advice might have been.

Example: A few months ago I had lost my second composition book of *Traces of You*. That was the second major setback because I had about ten stories in that book. I walked out on my job and went straight to my mother's house. I burst in the house and she could see instantly that something was wrong. I was so upset that I told her that I was going to quit my job and drive to California. *What would you say if your son or daughter told you some shit like that?* After she tried to reason with me and I wasn't listening she finally called me a coward. Those words stung to my heart but my mom knows how to be a mother. She threw the covers on herself (because she was still in the bed) and said, "Go you coward…I'm not going to shed no tears." She always knew how to throw that sarcasm in there. After I left for Chicago and about a week and a half later I remember standing at the bus stop listening to Marvin Sapp's, "Never would have made it." I became real doubtful about my journey and began to cry. I had to turn away from people just so they wouldn't see my tears. I text my mom and told her that I loved and missed her. She knows that I don't talk like that so instantly her "Mother Alarm" radar went up. She text me back, "*You are not a coward. I am so proud of you. Go all the way!*" Damn if that put a smile on my face mixed with tears. Now that's what I call bittersweet. Let me write that again…THAT'S WHAT I CALL BITTERSWEET. This book is for you…THANK YOU, MOM.

February 22nd

Today started off real decent. After taking my dad to work I stopped off at a friend's house and smoked some weed with them. As I listened to their conversation of the same thing that they were talking about years ago I suddenly became depressed. Their type of slump is the type of slump I would never want to be in. I started to feel claustrophobic. I had to get out of the car because it felt like the world was getting smaller. I came home, looked around my mother's house and got re-motivated. I began using my knowledge to search around. I started calling different bookstores to start setting up book signings. I called Mayor Dwight Jones to see how he could help me with my project. I made a to-do list of things that needed to be done. Some of my ideas are to go door to door, sit in Panera's bread selling books while I ate, and stopping people on the street. Pretty much…whatever it takes to make it was my ideas. I would go to sex parties, college tours, and churches. The only thing that I needed was a finished product.

Thank goodness I finally spoke to the graphic designer who was designing my cover who had been avoiding me for three days. I know that I'm moving 1000 beats a minute when it comes to my book but other people move at snail pace. I can't move too fast or be overly aggressive when I need someone to do something for me especially when they are hooking me up on the price. However, I will light fire under someone's ass when its time. The graphic designer told me that the cover is almost complete.

I met Kim B.L.U.N.T who has published her own books and is doing extremely well for herself. She came and spoke to me about some questions that I had with marketing. She was a true blessing. She said that I was making all the right moves. She said that the publishing company I chose was official and that she wanted me to deal with her printing company where she could get me more books for my money. She said that I reminded her of the passion that she once had. She said that whatever it is about me…I got it. This made me feel good. She almost cried twice after she saw all the work that I had already put in. She was very excited and told me that she would help me in any way she could.

This extra encouragement gave me a boost of energy. It's time for me to walk my path. To some people me being back at home mean I'm losing my footing and my passion. I promise that this is the calm before the storm. A finished product is almost ready. Oprah I haven't forgotten about you yet. I refocused and I'm about to come at you at triple speed. I'm not done by a long shot. I almost fell to tears seeing my future. I told my mom that I'm truly enjoying the struggle. I know that I'm going to make it but I'm taking my time enjoying every moment of it. In a sense…I'm enjoying being a nobody because I still have a sense of self; a part of myself that I don't ever want to lose focus on. In these primary stages I am as creative as I can be. I write freely with no boundaries, interviews, appointments or whatever there is to block the creative writing process. I am truly myself. Everyone wants to see the end results and see me fly over the world. I just pray that I stay true to myself. If the only reason why this book is out is to remind myself of the old me then, in my eyesight, this book has served its purpose.

2nd Entry

The day has ended in its most fashionable fashion. The book cover is complete and progress is really beginning. I'm almost out of money but my income check is about to come in. That is the last check that I will get. After that I am completely on my own…I'm ready. **To the Kids**: *when your back is against the wall fight harder than you've ever fought before…give it your all.* It's now my time. Now time to show the world what I can do…I'm ready world.

February 23rd

Ooooooohhhhh… it's getting close to release date. March 4th is right around the corner. I am on super hype mode. Today the website is officially up (www.tracesofyou.org). I would like to personally thank Katrina for all the help that she's given. She gave up two days to work on the website for free. She put together the Official website of *Traces of You*…Thank You for that.

Not the project but the actual book is almost back in my hands. The birth is almost here and I will be able to hold my baby in my hands. Now it all falls back to me selling my product. I got hooked up with Kim Blunt who sees my vision to the fullest. I promise to keep the enthusiasm going. She invited me to a literal explosion that she's putting together. March 26th is my come out date to showcase my book in Richmond. I plan to go city to city and state to state to promote this best-selling book. I plan on seeing the world on my own. 1st stop… I have to make is back to Chicago. I have a product now and my mental is in a different state. Now I have an official product with connections in that area. I can't be stopped. I won't be stopped. I don't know where to go from there but that's the cool part of life. I told people that I would go door to door selling my book. If I go to thirty doors and only sell two books then at least I made a profit.

To the kids: *When you believe in something let there be no obstacle great or small. You must be ready to go door to door, street peddling, or whatever it takes to pursue your dream. I use to be very conscious of how people looked at or judged me. But, once I understood individuality then I truly understood myself and so will you.*

I show excitement about my progress but once again I'm back at the starting line. It's time to show the world…yea I'm still excited…oh yea I have a new sight. I'm going to put out four books in one year starting with *Traces of You*. The countdown begins March 26th. Yea…to all you writers and authors out there…I'm moving at record speed. I plan to put a whole new twist to the way books are written. I can't even categorize *Traces of You*. It hits so many levels that I'm going to put a lot of pens to rest. I always wanted something that I was better than everybody else at and this is it. Writing is my gift and I will prove it by writing on things unheard of. I'm not trying to be cocky at all but the truth is just the truth. I promise to put my heart, blood, sweat, and tears in each piece of literature I write. I promise to keep my mind open to fresh ideas and will never be typecast as a one dimensional writer. I promise to never forget who I am and where I came from. I will always help people from my status down and never up. Even when the world thinks that I'm being an asshole I promise those things. I promise to take care of my family as a man should.

February 26ᵗʰ

I spent the last two days celebrating. The book is almost complete, website is done and a book signing approaching. Everything was actually feeling good until I received an email at 1:02 am this morning from Kingdom Regal publishing company. It read:

Greetings Mr. Goode; I pray that this note finds you well. Your book was scheduled to go to print with a four day turnaround. However based on a spiritual, moral and integral decision, Kingdom Regal will not be able to publish your book and has decided to terminate the contract. After the reading and editing of your book we have made a decision not to publish based on its contents, moving forward with the publishing will say that we agree with its contents in which some is very graphic in nature. As you know we are pastors and our company is a Christian publishing company therefore we had to draw the line and as I said that line was drawn based on the content of your book. All the best in finding a publisher.

I have a lot of mixed feelings about receiving this notification. My first reaction was anger. I called and talked to one of the owners who told me that she had completed seventy percent of the work but could and would not finish. This all meant that I would have to find a new publisher and have to pay them to complete the book. I was upset that they couldn't finish editing the last thirty percent. They continued to tell me that they were pastors and that my work would go against their nature. I respect people's values but if you're almost complete with the editing then finish what you started. Upon meeting Kingdom Regal I had told them that even though some of the material was graphic in nature it all ended in a love form. I attempted to explain to them the sociological perspective of *Traces of You*. I told them how I asked fifty people fifteen questions and that I received different personalities because people came from all walks of life. I respected their decisions (I really had no choice) and cut my ties.

To the Kids: *Allow me to reiterate Perseverance -Steady persistence in a course of action, a purpose, a state, in spite of difficulties, obstacles or discouragement...even when people don't believe or are not able to see your vision continue to be yourself. Stand up for yourself and what you believe in at all times. Your light will shine amidst the darkness.*

A close mutual friend told me that the publishing company told her that they did not like a line in my acknowledgements in which, "*I gave praise to God, Allah, Buddha and all other forces that kept my mental state conscious when it was unconscious.*" People always ask and judge me on my spirituality. People have gone as far as to call me a devil worshipper. Let me tell you what I believe; I believe that there are a lot of "Higher" powers pulling us together to move forward. I choose to not put a name on the force that drives us but rather give respect to all religions. I read a lot of literature on different religions and realize that they all coincide with each other in some way, shape or form. I truly believe that if the world respects each other's religions instead of attempting to force their own beliefs on each other then this world will be a much better place to live.

I believe that I am living through the blood of my ancestors and great monikers such as Martin Luther King Jr., Malcolm X, John F Kennedy and all of the great leaders that are no longer with us, as well as the living. I look at President Obama and know that all things are possible once you put your mind to it. Once you have faith in yourself then you can endure through the end. My ancestors showed me how to endure and continuously move forward to breaking the chains that life tends to wrap around our conscious state of mind. I always say that one of the hardest things to do is unlearn and I believe that to this day. People learned how to be a slave to their trade and accept what life throws at them.

I told the publishing company that *Traces of You* would have been completely different if I chose to only ask church people. If I had done that then *Traces of You* would have been very boring and cliché. I chose people walking on the streets, inside clubs, restaurants, parks etc. I wanted to use people in their rarest forms; when they were by themselves and comfortable. I never scrutinized people for the answers that were given and was actually impressed by a few of the answers that I received. I am not bitter because of the decision that Kingdom Regal chose but I am upset that they did not see the vision in its entirety and chose to be (in my mind) close-minded. *Traces of You* will move forward. I have been met with much disappointment on this road but I have been given more encouragement than disappointment.

People always ask me how I can write a book on love/relationships if I am not in one. I tell them that I am completely in love with my writing. With my art I have been happy, depressed, sad, hurt, bored and greatly appreciated. Writing truly understands my sporadic mind and allows me to say what I need to say when it's needed to be said. If I stop writing I know that it (pad and pen) will always be there for me when I return. It (pad and pen) does not expect me to put on some type of heir, nor does it expect me to attempt to impress anyone but myself. I believe that love is when you can give yourself unconditionally to someone/something else. I found that love in writing.

I need to give love to a few artist who helped me along on this path; Talib Kwali, Lauryn Hill, Fugees, Jay-z, Nas, Snoop Dogg, Coldplay, Pink Floyd, The Beatles, Michael Jackson, Gym Class Heroes, Daft Punk, Color Me Badd, Andre 3000, Bob Marley, Lil Wayne, Drake, Floetry, Jill Scott, John P. Kee, Kidz in the Hall, Lupe Fiasco, Lox, Little Brother, Notorious B.I.G, Roots, Rick Ross, Slum Village, Stevie Wonder, TLC, Eminem, The Doors, Maroon 5, The Verve, Goapele, Ratpack, Common, J.Dilla, D'angelo, Tupac, Alicia Keys, Bilal, Brandy, Bone Thug, In4redd (my brother who showed me how to chase a dream), and Eddie Murphy (yea Eddie...I remember your singing career). These are only a handful of artist that deserves recognition. They, and more, have inspired the hearts of millions. Music plays a very important significant role in everyone's lives. Music is nostalgic. It gives you the chance to remember moments in your lives. Music gives you the chance to reflect back and relive that experience. All in a second; music gives me the feeling that I can conquer the world and at the same time can cause depression in the most severe form. I understand those emotions and for those sole reasons I am truly in love with music.

To the Kids*: Find that vice that gives you energy and stick with it. Whether it is a role model, friend, religion, music, God...whatever your vice is hold on to it and remain focused.*

Chapter 4

I can proudly say that I am a positive black man.

March

March 1st

Wooooow…what a day! Damn what a day. This is one of those days that I try to tell people about. I am with a new publishing company. It only took me four days to find one but I found someone that really believes in my vision and dream so much that they are finishing the book for FREE. I have to tell you that it feels like I have the book deal of the century. These are the breaks that continuously falls in my lap my entire life. I went running today *(which is usually when I can open my mind and allow my thoughts to run wild)*.

I learned the lesson of shutting my mouth and listening. I listened to every word of encouragement or discouragement that any person has ever given to me. I recanted to people telling me that I was destined for greatness. I listened to the people who told me that I was different and rebelled against all rules. I listened to the people who told me that I was bipolar, ADHD or just plain crazy. If I did not have all these "disorders" then I wouldn't be able to insert myself in all types of different projects, groups or whatever. I listened and understood that these are the things that make me…me.

I always hated when people tell me that I'm running away from something. I tell them that I can't run from something but only towards something. A runner does not run because there are other runners behind them. They run because they see the finish line. I see the finish line and see it getting closer and closer.

***To the Kids:** Don't believe in labels. Don't ever let people label you. I like to use Nicki Minaij as an example. All the problems that you've heard about her…as a kid if she was diagnosed and medicated, then she would not be the person that she is today. She's comfortable with herself which makes her stand out. You have to learn to be comfortable with yourself in order to shine. You have to know your weaknesses and strengths in order to know where you will excel in life. You knowing you does not start in school or in a gang but rather inside of yourself. So I tell you to not believe in labels that people attempt to put on you. Be Yourself.*

My book deal is beautiful. They are going to publish my book for free and I have my first book signing on March 26th. My name is actually on a flyer. The person who is holding the book signing, Kim Blunt is also directing a movie and after hearing that I directed my first movie she wants me to assist her. Her dedication to me helps fuel my motivation to assist her. I want to be able to get my hands in as many projects as I can. I want to learn the game in its entirety. I want to be universal and stretch my mind to infinite possibilities. I feel as though nothing can stop me.

For my book signing table I will have all types of trinkets to make my table stand out. I'm going to have wrist bands, key chains, cake gems and pens to entice people to come to my table. I know that the book is good but I believe in overselling my product. I am a fan of subliminal messages. If people have a key chain wherever they go people will see it and the visual of the key chain will get stuck in their head. When they see the book the subconscious part of their brain will kick in and they will remember the book cover. I know that these are good marketing strategies. This is the kind of aggressive attitude I've always possessed when I go after things in life whether it be women, jobs or whatever. I never noticed this side of me until one night a friend of mine (when I was living in a house) told me that his cousin's house had been raided and we could get whatever the police did not take. I tried my best to take everything I could (ha-ha). Even the stuff that was nailed down. I even took the screen door. I started putting that screen door up as soon as we got back at 4 in the morning. My friend went to sleep and woke up at 6am and saw me still putting the screen door together. He asked me where I got my energy from. I don't know where it comes from but once I become focused on something there is absolutely nothing that can stop me. I become fixated on that one project and I don't stop until I feel like it's complete. People call that determination. I guess if that's what determination is then I'm full of it. I feel that as a man you should complete every project that you put your mind to.

I'm constantly asked about love. I understand what love is. I understand that love is keeping "that" person in clear view…Never forgetting who they are internally. Never forgetting what drew you to "that" person and at the same time continuously growing in your own life. In a way I took all of these reasons and turned them inward *(that's why people call me selfish)* but I learned that you need to guard your heart. Your heart needs to be guarded like a fortress because whoever breaks it takes a small piece of you. The more times you put your heart up gives other people a chance to take a part of your soul away. I guard mine because I'm afraid of getting hurt. I put my love in my writing. I pour all my emotions in my writing because I feel like this (pad and pen) is the only vice that truly understands me. My writing consumes me.

Traces of You is almost alive. I'm going to break all types of barriers with this one. I'm getting ready for the world and advise the world to get ready for me. I'm rocking doo-rags to get the waves back. I'm back in the gym so I can have the body on point. I'm getting re-focused. I plan on selling my book in record numbers in my first week; I plan to direct my second movie soon, Website is up, publicity is on point and the Road to Oprah is alive. Yoooo....the focus is on 1000 right now. Whatever I got is clearly appealing. I'm calling this shit out like Babe Ruth used to call out his homeruns. I pointed my hands to the stars and I'm heading to it at full steam. Listen to me...I called stardom since I 1st started this project and I'm proving it to you. Everything I said I was going to do I did it. I love the fact that my words hold power. When I tell people that I'm going to do something they believe me.

Oprah, I'm coming at you full steam and there is nothing that can stop me. Don't take this as me being impatient either; I am truly enjoying the struggle because every new day is a surprise. I knew I wouldn't be an overnight superstar so I'm sitting back enjoying every moment of it. The name of this book is Road to Oprah. I'm enjoying the ride all the way to the top. I almost don't want to get on the show because that means I would have to end this book. I just want you to truly understand that I'm enjoying the ride. I'm respecting every door that gets slammed in my face because I know that soon enough one of them is going to open.

I would personally like to thank each and every person that helped to make Traces of You. Every person in that book has given me the energy to push forward. It is their stories that made Traces of You possible. You 50 are the reason why "Road to Oprah" is so valuable. I pushed that book on the sole fact that I felt every one of your stories deserved a chance to be heard. Pause: I apologize for the stories that did not make Traces of You. I lost two of my composition books and do not want you to feel as though I left you out. Play: I feel that each and every person in my book are worthy of their stories being told. I don't know what drew me to you but I was drawn. I don't specifically have a favorite story because each and every one of you meant something special to me. You 50 have truly been an inspiration to me. Thank you for being the truly unique person that you are. You 50 have given me glimpses in your lives that you only reserve for your family and close friends. Thank you...*Traces of You* and *Road to Oprah* is here...only two more books before I reach my quota of four books in one year. Watch my swag.

March 3rd

Damn I woke up in a beautiful mood. I had a great night sleep and woke up with my brain on fire. I did two documentaries for my YouTube channel and its only 12:30 pm. My brain is on fire. It feels good when my brain is awake. I have two more documentaries to do today and I'm getting amped. When my book drops I plan to hit barbershops and beauty salons 2-3 times a day. I'm enjoying the marketing mode. It feels different and gives me a chance to meet all walks of life. I love hearing other people talk about their dreams, art and lifestyle. I love meeting new people and selling my own book gives me the opportunity to do just that...meet new people. I think making YouTube videos is a hot idea.

My sister and I talked this morning about how I felt about being back in Richmond at home. I told her that being home is my kryptonite. At home I have family, food and television; all the things that make me weak at my art (writing). But then I told her that my life is also being played like a movie. If I was to die right now then I would be okay with that because that would be the end of the movie. Every step I take is progress and I'm supposed to enjoy every moment of it until the curtains close. Even though home is my kryptonite I'm enjoying every second of it. I'm getting mentally and physically prepared for the next scene. I must tell you the purpose of my YouTube videos. I'm going to turn them into a mini movie and give them away with this book *"Road to Oprah."* I'm preparing for the future. It feels good to prepare for the future. Even if *Traces of You* completely fails I already know that I'm putting out a second book. That's the aggressive mind frame that I'm in. It's either writing or nothing.

My home-girl just informed me that my book is officially copy written. Yea...I hadn't even gotten the book copy written yet but now its official (Thanks, B). I told you, today is a good day (Thank you, Ice Cube) and I'm still zoning because the day is not over yet.

To the Kids: Learn to enjoy the little things. On your road things will get tough…situations will get hard but enjoy the curve balls that life throws at you and learn how to smile when it's time to smile but remain focused…that is called humility. Learn how to stay focused even when all the praise is upon you. Don't live in the past but rather embrace the future.

I would like to thank each and every person who is reading *"Road to Oprah."* If you are continuing to read this then you are truly interested in the mind of Raymond Goode. It means that you want to know how I think as well as my actions. I'm giving you (the reader) *traces of me* that I show to no one. I'm baring my soul in each word and phrase that I say. This means that you are the truest of fans. I thank you for your dedication and even if it's not authentic…*Goode Raymond*…I just autographed each and every book that is read. Thank you for being a fan of the Raymond Goode show. *(It's hard work being me…ha-ha).*

March 5th

I had a breakdown night last night. I feel the pressure of home responsibilities. It feels like I'm consistently surrounded by people. People I love but I'm not getting a chance to breathe. I love those times that I have no phone, no friends and no distractions. I call it my "me day." It's that one day that I can be alone and make any decision that I want. It's my mental stress free day.

To the Kids: Find a way to make time for yourself. Locate a cubbyhole, corner in your room, park bench or whatever gives you the opportunity to get lost in your own thoughts. Many of your friends/family will throw their problems your way that you won't have time to focus on your own problems. Learn to mentally free yourself from your environment and you will learn to work on your own problems. If you can't fix your own problems then it will be impossible to fix anyone else's. Even if you can only get away for fifteen minutes a week it will make a difference.

I woke up this morning feeling refreshed. I spoke to a friend from Philadelphia (Dajuan Diggs) whom I hadn't talked to in years. He told me that he was proud of my progress and that he was watching my YouTube channel. I thanked him and promised that I would shed some light to his non-profit organization called, Focus on Father. Focus on Fathers is a voluntary program that provides direct services through parenting education, case management, and peer support services for fathers, stepfathers, and adult males who are involved in raising children. He told me that they visited prisons and worked with fathers in the surrounding areas. I pray that I shed some light to your program brother and encourage you to continue. I am very proud of you and continue your struggle to keep your family together as well as the families surrounding you. If there's anything I can do to assist just dial me up. Dajuan told me that I did very well in front of a camera (little does he know that I'm scared every time I turn that damn thing on) and that he wanted me to come to Philadelphia to sell some of my books with the possibility of speaking at one of their conventions. I believe this is a positive program that I am comfortable enough and willing to attach my name to. I am heavily concerned about the mentality of males (especially African American males) who are lost at being fathers and think that things would be better if they were not in the household at all. I don't have to be a father to understand the importance of having a father figure (Strong father figure) in the household. I told Dajuan that (with *Traces of You*) I didn't know my whereabouts in June but if I could make it I would.

I did another documentary for my YouTube channel. It feels good putting people on camera. I like how people are nervous about talking and eventually become comfortable with the camera's rolling. I tell people to be honest and be themselves and they shouldn't have anything to worry about. I remember one time when my friends and I had went to an Allen Iverson birthday bash in Maryland and this woman interviewed us about what we thought about the party. (I had a few drinks that night so I was already in a rare mode). After the interview I told her that I thought her job was easy and that I thought I could do it. (She got really mad about that hahaha). My friend later told me that my comment was disrespectful. I told him that I was only being truthful and I really did think her job was easy. That's the way I think. I truly believe that if I put my mind to something then I can accomplish that goal. I went to school for one or two semesters and the only thing that I learned was that I can learn anything on my own. That is the purpose of libraries, bookstores and internet. When I want to learn something I will spend countless hours in bookstores and/or libraries reading and taking notes. They are completely free to utilize and I can read all the material I want to. I will look up every word that I don't know and write it down so I would know what it meant the next time I came across that word. I would have notebooks written of words and since I always forget the word I was always flipping through that notebook. When I got to a subject that I didn't understand I would call around and usually someone knew someone who knew what I was trying to know. I promote school heavily but if you can't self motivate and stay focused then school will never work for you.

To the Kids: People who hunt for diamonds spend months and even years looking for that one piece of crystal. They sift through dirt and mud most of the time coming up empty handed. But once one single diamond is found then they all rejoice and laugh. After the hype they are right back to work. That is the same way education is. A lot of times you will be frustrated with your schoolwork; you will go to tutors, stay after class and things will still not click but you have to continue to work on that problem…never give up. Eventually the problem will work itself out and it will feel the same as if you had found that diamond. You will laugh, kick yourself and call yourself stupid for not figuring it out sooner. The main thing is that you stayed focused and didn't give up. You figured out the gem but the real diamond was all the hard work that you put in.

March 7th

A good day…had a few drinks to celebrate so I'm feeling real good right now. First of all I would like to thank Margaret Wade who has assisted me with marketing by making *Traces of You* key chains, bookmarks and my *Traces of You* coat. You have been a huge help to me while I chase this dream to the ground. I watched some of the documentaries that I did from my family who told me that I never should have left my jobs and that I should have stayed in Virginia and chased my dream. I'm truly happy that my family has the balls to say those things and they don't always agree with my decisions. I call that real family love. My family sees my vision and encourages me at the same time calling me a fool. I've run short of money…let me rephrase that…I'm out of money. The bank reads a negative balance but I have my income check coming in this Friday. After that check (financially) I will be on my own. *Traces of You* will be my main source of income.

March 9th

Beautiful day. The tax place forgot to send my income return in and gave me forty dollars back for their mistake. My friend sent me two hundred dollars which allowed me to keep my phone on. These are the strange things that happen to me all the time. When my back is against the wall things mysteriously work out. I was starting to get nervous about the publication of my book. I hadn't heard from Kim (author, publisher) in almost a week. But I received a text from her stating that her grandma and uncle had died on the same day. I would like to take the time to send my condolences to Kim Blunt and her family who I know is going through it right now. I feel your pain. I lost an aunt and uncle in the same week and even though I felt the pain; I felt it more because I knew that my family was feeling it the hardest.

I see other people's problems around me and it makes my problems seem so insignificant. Other's people's issues are the things that keep my mind at reality. When I hear people complain about their jobs or what they "could" do to make their lives better I usually don't care. People say I have a heart of stone which is not the case at all. I simply don't care about the minor problems that people face on a day to day basis. I care about the woman in the projects who can't feed her children. I care about the female victim in the Dunbar rape case (Florida) where so many guys raped her, forced her to have oral sex on her son and poured household chemicals inside of her to remove the evidence of DNA. I care about the soldier at war who can't and hasn't seen his/her family in months or even years. I care about the things that people should care about.

I don't worry about the problems right in front of me because I truly believe that the problems that I see can and will work themselves out. This is one of the reasons why I have problems with the welfare system and the mentality of some of my African American men and women. Truth be told, being stuck inside the "system" gives people a false sense of being secure. They accept their monthly checks from the government and live in low income housing. They accept what is given to them and can't see past the problems outside of their doors. They become a prodigy of their environment and stop looking for the "more" in life. People can't see past their own problems let alone understand problems on a global scale. I'm not talking about all the people in the system because I truly believe that some people don't want to live in that situation forever but I am talking about a vast majority.

I was at the store recently and this fourteen year old girl told me that her grandma was really sick and she needed a ride *(a few streets down)* to see her. I obliged and as soon as I pulled off she said, "I want you to know that I'm not sucking your dick." I was completely taken back because it was then I realized that this was the life that she lived. I hate the fact that women feel as though the only way to make money is to sell their bodies for 20-40 dollars. Women *(especially black women)* are the queens of the earth and have more to offer than lying on their backs or their knees. I tried to give her some knowledge of self and saw that it went in one ear and out the other. I could tell that so many people have tried to help her and I was put in that category. I hope I planted a seed. Every time I see her at that store the first thing she says is, "I'm not prostituting" which I know that she is. I gave her a book that I kept in my car. I told her that I couldn't stop her from doing what she was going to do but she needed to read. I told her that whenever she was idle she needed to be reading. Education in any form is a good form. I hope I planted a seed. I saw her two weeks later and she ran to my car and whipped that book out of her back pocket. I stopped hoping…I knew I had planted a seed. That young girl is who I care about.

To the Kids: You are the future and education is the key. I don't always preach about school but rather the education of life. You have to educate your mind and see above the system. Utilize the mirror image technique. Stand in front of a mirror and ask yourself questions. No matter how stupid the questions seem continue to ask. "If I carry this gun what's the consequences?" "If I sell my body what is the negative that can come from it?" "What do people think of my pants sagging?" Once you continuously ask and answer these questions they will eventually turn into "what is my purpose in life?" Those are the questions that will make you mature mentally.

One of the first steps in marketing *(once I have the book in hand)* is that I'm going to invite my entire family out to eat *(of course I'm paying)* and I will give each of them five books. *(I'm going for the "already made it" approach)*. With me paying for dinner will give the illusion that I'm already on the way to the top. I will give them a time frame of four days. *(In my family if they hold the money too long then they will spend it)*. My family is full of hustlers who can sell anything from drugs to junk. I truly believe that they can hustle five books. The family members that I get ALL my money back from I know I can trust with another shipment. The ones who don't give me all my money has to be kept on a shorter leash. I'll never cut family off because it is a combination of them which makes me. I know the money from those sales will generate more money than I put out for dinner. Plus it will let them know that they are a part of this dream as well.

I just realized what progress means to me. I hear people say that they are proud of the progress I've made in the past year but let me show you my progress. As a child *(around six months to two years old)* I wasn't allowed to go outside. I got older and went outside but wasn't allowed to go out of the yard. I got a little older and could go around the neighborhood by myself but had to be in before the street lights came on. I got older and I could venture throughout the entire city and now I'm all over the world…that's what I call progress. Most people measure my steps from a few years ago and I measure my steps from the time of birth.

To the Kids: Don't believe in boundaries…continue to break them in leaps and bounds. The word graduation means that you transitioned from something but it also means that you've transitioned to something else. Don't allow people to put restraints on your lives and tell you where you should stop at. Grow and make mistakes because those mistakes add up to growth.

March 11th

Today was a beautiful day. I'm in marketing mode and I just received my *Traces of You* key chains which I plan to give away with the books. I put another YouTube video out, wrote a chapter for my third book and went on a two mile run. What's your day like? Mine is real. Everything signed and sealed. (Thanks Beanie Siegel). The day the book hits my hand I'm off and running. It will feel like a leash has been taken off the dog. I told my mom that when I'm running (around the neighborhood) it feels like I'm free…it's only me and the outside world. That song by Lupe Fiasco was playing and I had zoned out on the lyrics. I understood the words when he raps the song Kick Push. Kicking is a downward motion and pushing is a vertical motion. Once you start moving freely all the problems are behind you. That song played in my head (as I ran) and I stopped in the middle of my run and turned around. There was no one behind me. There was no one cheering me on to continue the run...only me. I understood Kick Push because my run allows me to be me without any distractions. I follow this analogy wherever I go. I feel like no one can cheer for me like I can cheer for me. I continue to kick and push. I continue to strive for more...for better. I can't stop pushing because every step is getting closer and closer to my dream. I still continue to run to clear my head. LISTEN UP WORLD...whenever you see me running I'm clearing my head from all the negative thoughts and allowing fresh ideas to come through. That is when I'm at my most dangerous mode (ha-ha).

I need to give a huge shout out to Richmond V.A. I will always carry you with me and I am a firm believer in giving back to the community. I fully plan to create new jobs and bring new businesses to the city. I will invest in black owned businesses and give people a chance to fulfill their lifelong dreams. No matter how far I go I will continue to give back to the city that has had my full support since day one. As a matter of fact I have the V.A. state flag tattooed over my heart. I love my city because I see the potential that it has. I see the same dream that Neverett Eggleston (owner of Croaker Spot) envisioned. He is truly a part of our black history.

A friend of mine called and told me that he wanted me to participate in assistance with his catering business. He wants to give away his appetizers as I sell my books. The more I push the more doors are starting to open. It feels good stepping in the game with people that are hungry like me. Someone told me something was obviously wrong with me since I am 32 and not married. I didn't really know what to say to that. I like to think that when the love of a woman catches my heart then I will know. Right now I'm still finding things out about myself. Peeling back the layers and getting to know myself is a hard but fun job. I'm seeing characteristics that other people see in me. I've always said that I can't see myself; I can't see how other people view me. I tell people that I do things because they seem right to me. But now I'm actually seeing the elements that people have been telling me my whole life.

I'm elevating into the man that I want to be and not the one everyone expects me to be. I'm maturing at record speed. They always say that girls mature faster than boys…I must agree with them. Don't worry, people still say that I'm immature as hell and I can't deny that either. I still have a lot of growing to do but I think I'm moving in the right direction. *Pause: I still won't grow up. I'm a grown ass kid. Swear I should be locked up for all the stupid shit that I did….Thanks Kanye West. That line is still one of my mottos. Play:*

HEY YOU…the reader…thank you for being a part of the Raymond Goode Show. Let me show you the breakdown of my books. *Traces of You* is my baby. The concept of the book is ingenious. That book will inflict differing emotions inside the reader. That book will get me on talk shows, newspapers and radio shows. My interviews will intrigue the masses enough to pick up *Road to Oprah*. *Road to Oprah* will either give you the option of thinking if I'm absolutely fucking crazy or a genius (*which is a very thin line if I must say so myself*). *Road to Oprah* will make you desire my military book. The 1st two books combined with my personality will make you wonder what I could write in my military book. My fourth book will be my mini-series project. It's going to be hood and my plan is to actually start filming my first television series (*If I'm not already on that path*). You have to realize my determination. I'm chasing a dream which I will chase as far as I can. I'm not after the money but I'm testing how far I can push my brain and body. People say I show passion about what I'm doing and I tell them that's because I care about every single word that I put on paper. I am opening my life to scrutiny and criticism. I pour complete emotions on paper. You already have your opinion about me and I respect that. Whether you think I'm crazy or a genius the honest truth is I simply don't care…I'm me.

March 12th

What a beautiful day. I'm sitting outside with a mixed drink and allowing the cool breeze to brush past my face. It feels good to allow my brain to relax. Someone told me a long time ago that when you look up at the sky you think happy thoughts and when you look down you think negative thoughts. Subconsciously I find myself always looking up. You know what I like about the game (industry game) I'm coming in being completely me. I haven't changed my values or opinions. A lot of artists have to change (or think that they have to change) who they are as a person to make it. A lot of people in the industry lose out on their core values because they are afraid to show who they really are. I call that a sellout. Anytime a person has to sell out the things that they believe in or order to make a dollar is called a true sell out. *(Selling out and comprising is two completely separate things)*. This means that the artist would sell bullshit to the community in order to seek personal gain. I pray that as I move up in the world; I will never lose out on the sense of who I am and what it means to help people. Like I said before I always plan to help people from my level down and never up. Some things I will never sell myself short on.

I tell people that I don't care about money and that is the truth. I hate what money does to a person and how it makes them react to situations. For the love of money people will kill their own people, it will make females lay on their backs, it causes world destruction. Money is only a piece of paper. To me it's not even worth the piece of paper it's printed on. I know you may ask yourself why I'm pushing myself so hard. On one hand I know the steps needed in order to "make it." Words are powerful and that is how you capitalize the game. Here is an example: You may not know how to do a job but if you use the right words then you will impress the interviewer enough that they will want to give you a chance. I learned how to use my words. I'm also pushing so hard because I believe that every person has a story to tell in some way shape or form and their story should be told.

I believe in a dream; I believe in something bigger than me. On the flip side; I hear so many conversations on the end of the world in 2012. I hear these conversations in coffee shops, bars, schools and homes. I wonder if people really believe that the world will end and if so how come they don't push to fulfill their wildest dreams. Ma$e had a song titled, "If I had 24hrs to live" and in a sense if the world is going to end in 2012 then I feel as though I am living my 24 hrs. I encourage people who truly believe in the 2012 myth to live life to the fullest. Let me make this clear…I am not saying that I believe in the 2012 myth but if it is then I'm going to have my fun and enjoy it to the fullest. When I almost committed suicide last year; Raymond Goode (in a sense) died. What you see is a man that had one foot in the grave and now that I've taken it out I see a new world in front of me. I hear other people's problems but I face new problems that they can't even see. It feels like I'm all alone in this world sometimes but at the same time I am eerily calm.

People always ask me why I enjoy being alone so much. People don't understand the type of problems that I face which is the reason why I write. This pad and this pen is the only vice that understands me completely. That is why I pour my heart in every word that I write down. This is the only place I can be myself at. When I write I show depression, sorrow, hate, anger, happiness, sadness, cocky, arrogance, fear, introvert, extrovert and every other emotion that I have. The only thing closer to me pouring my heart on this paper is me cutting my veins and allowing the blood to drop over theses lines. This is me.

I did a shout out YouTube video to my cousin Michael Archer or D'Angelo as you might know him. He is my cousin as long as the blood is blue in our veins. We had a falling-out a few years ago. I must tell you the story in my eyesight. He may say something different but this is how I saw it. I, my dad and my uncles were doing a tree job in a fairly decent "white" neighborhood when he (Michael) pulled up in his hummer (you know me...I was excited to see him) but he came off so raw...so different. There was an older white guy walking his dog down the street minding their own business when Michael snapped on him saying, "What's up son...you copasetic son?" The white man was so nervous that he picked up his pace and continued to face forward. Then he (Michael) told me to take a drink with him because he had a bottle of Remy in the hummer.

I took a drink with him and when I asked for a second drink he snapped on me.

"Goddamn son...every time I come to Virginia niggas always begging for shit," he said. I was shocked and taken back from his response. I was fucking pissed. I grabbed his plastic cup from off of his hummer and threw it across the street.

"Now go pick it up," Michael told me.

"Nigga I ain't never begged you for shit and I'm not go'n pick it up unless you apologize," I yelled at him. He told me that a real man doesn't apologize for shit and that he wasn't going to apologize. I went to pick up his cup and flung that muthafucker as far as my arm would allow it to go. After that we stood glaring at each other in silence. In my head I thought that he was the older cousin testing the strength of the younger cousin. I still had no idea that he was dead serious.

"Is we cool…is this shit over with?" I asked him

"Nigga fuck you," he told me. I was finally over the top I told him

"Don't forget…you're industry…I'm still in the streets…I know where you live muthafucker," I told him and walked off. We hadn't talked for over a year and I received a phone call a year later with him apologizing about the situation. We made amends I mean hey…we're family.

People continuously ask me why I don't use my cousin to get where I want to be. The reason being: Michael Archer (D'Angelo) is his own man with his own set of problems. I am very proud of his accomplishments and his achievements. Even if we don't talk on a regular basis he's still family and we will be whether he has money or not. Plus I truly believe that *Traces of You* is good enough to fly all by itself. I know *Traces of You* has longevity and has the energy to fly high. It's my baby. Michael, I feel as though you didn't help anyone in the family so I chose not to reach out to you. I know that with your involvement with *Traces of You* I would soar to the top a lot faster than I anticipate but I refuse to humble myself to ask. But please don't get it twisted. I love your songs and thought every C.D. you put out was HOTTTTT. I was riding with this female the other day and (once she found out you was my cousin) started digging in with questions about your drinking and attempting to buy a prostitute. Even though we haven't talked in a while I still won't let anyone head bash family. I cut the conversation short. As long as the blood is blue in my vein you will always be my family. I hope you don't take this entry as disrespect in any way but if you did the truth is just the truth. When I make it to the top we can still get a drink…we'll make a toast. Love you, Cuzzo.

March 14th

What a day…What a day. I went to my publicist house and the book is going at full speed right now…1000 miles per minute. I was really afraid about the length of the book and if it would be big enough to officially call it a book. I was stressing that it would only be 100 pages or so. Nooooo!!!! It's going to be over 400 pages. I am going to sell the fuck out of this book. The publicist told me that she has never seen my style of writing before. I told her that I'm going to be something special and that she has never met a person like me before. I'm ready to show the world what Raymond Goode can do. I plan to shoot a commercial for *Traces of You* and put it on YouTube. I'm about to get ridiculous. The commercial will corner the market. I can't even tell you what the commercial will be about but you will soon see. March 26th is the official book signing and I will bring everything I know to this project. I hope y'all can tell the excitement as I write it.

I heard the word narcissism thrown around about me a lot lately. I didn't know what it meant so I looked it up. The term narcissistic is often used as pejoratives, denoting vanity, conceit, egotism or simple selfishness. That definition doesn't agree with me. I see the truth as the truth is. *Traces of You* is a hot project. When I'm asked about my book it gives me shivers. It sparks something in me that I've never felt before. I feel empowered. The female later told me that being narcissistic was not necessarily a bad thing it just meant that I was passionate about my work.

Today I went to see my grandmother in the hospital. She had a slight heart attack recently. She is my heart and is one of the main reasons why *Traces of You* must survive. She is the rock of my family. She has built a legacy to be respected. You have no idea what kind of family I have. We argue and fuss but every Sunday we come together at my grandmother's house to play basketball, throw horseshoes, drink and smoke, play cards, dominoes, fight and at the same time remain a strong family unit. She has built a family that no one has ever seen before and it is my plan to keep this family a unit. She is the reason why I gave a large part of the *Traces of You* acknowledgements to her because I feel as though she deserved it. My promise to her is to keep all of my uncles, aunts, cousins, nieces and nephews as crazy as they can be as well as keep the love going strong. I will make sure we get together every holiday, social gathering, birthday or whatever. I can't replace her but I will play my part in keeping this family together. I won't ever let anyone go so far that they can't be pulled back.

Pause: I see your vision grandma. I swear to God I see your vision and I will uphold it to the fullest. I must dedicate this song to you grandma because it helps to ease the tears that are streaming down my face right now… "For the Love of You" by the Isley Brothers. This is the song that I dedicate to you. Play:

My grandma would always play old school music whenever one of her friends died so my next musical artist dedications are going to be dedicated to my grandmother. I would like to thank Al Green, Sly Stone and the Family, Marvin Gaye, Sam Cooke, Isley Brothers, Four Tops, The Emotions, Ben E. King, Percy Sledge, Rose Royce, Temptations, Diana Ross and the Supremes, Tina Turner, James Brown, Ray Charles, Jackson Five, Otis Redding, Bill Withers, Smokey Robinson and the Miracles, Commodores, Gladys Knight and the Pips, Harold Melvin and the Blue Notes, LTD, Barry White, The Main Ingredients, Teddy Pendergrass, Bloodstone, Manhattans, Curtis Mayfield, The Chi-lites, The Delfonics, the Dells, The O'Jays, Earth Wind and Fire, Eddie Floyd, Clarence Carter and Heatwave.

Pause: Grandma you are truly a part of black history. You have managed to keep a black family together under all circumstances. No matter how dysfunctional people think we are…we are still a family. Whenever I talk about black history it will be your name that I bring up. We are a family bound by love. Play:

I talked to my cousin, Jabari Cox/Goode who told me, "Yo when I read your articles…no homo…it gives me goose bumps." Now, that put me in a different frame of mind. He said he didn't think that I was crazy and I should continue to push for my goal. In that one sentence he told me how proud he was of me. It sent chills down my spine. He wasn't concerned about the money, because he knows that I'm going to make it, but he was proud that his cousin's name was in the newspaper (for something good of course…not the gotcha paper). That makes me feel good when I know the love is genuine. He's too hood to talk like that so I know it came from the heart.

March 15th

I'm getting amped for next week. I'm having a few difficulties with getting the book published but I got people working around the clock to get it out. The first printing company is too backed up for me to get my order filled by the 26th. They were only going to charge me three dollars per book but since they are backed up; I have to go for a quick fix and go with this company called 48 hour books. The difference is that they are going to charge me seven dollars per book. I really don't care about the costs because I just want my book in my hand so I can go to work. With the first printing company I was only going to spend three hundred dollars which is all I have to my name but now the books are going to be around 450.

I really didn't know how I was going to get the money but when I don't stress that's when things work itself out. My dad gave me fifty dollars tonight which is really huge. This is how things work out for me. I know the rest will come so there's no reason to stress. My publicist told me that she was really enjoying reading my stories and since she's doing it for free I know it's the truth. I guess I'm supposed to be hype but I still need that book in hand. I'm growing tired of shooting videos and telling people that I'm writing a book. I'm ready to produce. My fans are ready to see me produce…yes I said fans.

My past still follows me. I was involved in a fight. It irritates me that at the age of 32 I'm telling you I was involved in a fight but two dudes were about to jump my friend. They attempted to jump him even after they agreed that it was only going to be a one on one fight. I told them to shoot the ones (that means fight one on one). People don't fight fair anymore but run to guns and knives. Excuse my French but that's a pussy move. I love a good one on one street fight. That's when you can get it in and get it over with. When I saw the other guy attempting to hit my boy I was not about to let it ride like that. Of course you know that I'm a one hitter quitter (that means I hit and he quit…ha-ha). I know I still do dumb shit but some things are embedded in me. I can't let a man take a beat down if I can help it.

March 19th

I know I haven't written in a few days but I've been busy with getting the book together. My publicist told me some of the problems that she sees in my writing. She wants me to learn how to edit my own books. I think it's a good trade to learn. It's a learning experience that I am truly enjoying. I spent 18 hours damn near straight editing my own book. My friend and business partner, Bianca taught me the trick of using text to talk. I'm letting the words be read back to me aloud. That is a great learning tool for me. I'm able to see where commas and periods are supposed to go. I am really proud of myself for learning something new. Things are not hard once I start focusing on it. I don't have the (text to talk) software on my computer but I camped out at her house to do it. I suppose that's what you call determination.

To the Kids: Stay determined in any course of action. Whatever seems like an obstacle; learn how to get over it. When you show determination people will notice. When you see your peer has received an 'A' you have to think of how that person received that 'A.' That means they went home and studied. While at lunch they are thinking of answers. It takes a lot to earn a good grade. Each and every one of you has the determination to make the Grade. It all depends on how bad you want it.

An update on my grandma: She had the triple bypass surgery and is recovering. She is still in ICU but we're monitoring her daily. The general census that I've heard from the family is that they all wonder about the breakdown of the family once she passes. I want to say that adds more pressure to the *Traces of You* project, which it does but somehow I stay eerily calm. Like I said before I understand the vision that my grandmother has and when she does pass I need to be ready to play my part to keep this family alive. I think that everyone focuses so hard on the negative thoughts that nothing but positive things can come from it. MY FAMILY WILL SURVIVE. *Note to self: On this Road to Oprah I have experienced a lot.*

I pray that the world sees the difference between my book and other authors. Daily I'm giving you a front row seat to how my mental switches on a regular basis. I can't wait to hit the road again. Woooow…last year I was ready to commit suicide and this year I'm on top of my game. Damn I love life. I can't explain the mood I'm in right now. *Traces of You* is my suit.

The Army and Navy was a suit that I put on to make me a better person. Afterwards I became a Jr. Correctional Officer at a facility. The hours were great and the pay was good but I became bored with it. Next, I put on the suit of being a group home counselor. That job felt great. I came in with no degree and within three months I was the Sr. Recreational Counselor in charge of seventeen personnel and seventeen group homes from Richmond Va. all the way to Newport News. That job led me to In-Home counseling which I made up my own hours and had the thrill of meeting kids all throughout the Richmond area. That job gave me the opportunity of putting on the suit of Day Treatment which was the icing on the cake. With all three jobs combined I was at a grand total of $90,000 a year. These were all the suits that were given to me and I stepped in each one excelling at each position. But my mind began to wonder on piecing together my own suit. I wanted a suit that I designed for myself. I put the *Traces of You* suit together. I pieced it myself and I plan to stand tall and proud in it.

Now, let me talk to the media for a minute. Listen up…I know who I am before I even walked in the game so it don't matter what you say or write about me because I know who I am. No matter what you write in your papers or reports nor what you say on your talk shows about me; I will remain the same. You can't change me or my decisions. I really don't care what you say because I'm going to keep it real at all times. But I want you to remember that my mom is watching and listening to every word that you say, on that note I will ask for mercy but don't push my back into a wall. I don't like to show anger and you really don't want to see that side of me. I'm an animal when I show my teeth (ha-ha).

March 21st

The nervousness is starting to set in. The book is beginning to take flight. My publicist and friend are almost finished with editing the book. Another one of my friends is almost finish with the book cover (*he said he would be done by the end of the day*). I talked to 48 hours (publishing company) who told me that the book will have to be in by 11am march 22. That means once it goes into print I am completely on my own. Now all the talking and traveling that I did will come to a head. Please don't let me forget the key chains and the cake blow pops that I will have by this Friday. I'm going to set up my table and have it looking really nice. I talked to this guy name Marquis who told me that he would shoot *Traces of You* commercials for only 25 dollars a shoot. I also met a critic. He told me that he didn't see my vision. He didn't see why I left Virginia (the manner that I did) to try and get on the Oprah show. He also said that he didn't understand the purpose of the book. Even after I explained it to him several times he said that he just didn't understand. I finally had to do a synopsis on him *(asking him a few questions and doing a verbal story on the spot)*. I had to make him see my vision. I don't think he fully understood my vision but he told me that he would support me regardless. I like the fact that he's a critic. I know I can't make everyone see things my way but I will give it my all. I respect his views and opinions just as I will respect the rest of the world's views and opinions.

It is now the wee hours of the morning…about 2am on 3/22 but since I haven't been to sleep yet I will write this entry under 3/21. I just finished putting the final touches on *Traces of You*. I learned how to put it in PDF form and my guy is still working on the cover. Everyone and everything is coming together on the project and it's still pretty much free.

I would like to give a huge shout out to a good friend, Bianca Brown who gave up her only two days off of work in order to edit the second half of my book. *Pause: Stop second guessing yourself. You have talents and skills that you don't see but they are there. You are a strong beautiful woman and the devil comes in all shapes and sizes. You will excel in all that you do. Believe in yourself and I will always support you.*

I also want to give a shout out to my friends *(homeboys as I like to call them)* and I use that word very tightly. Today, I was with the squad and I got in the mood to write. One, I couldn't find a pen and when I asked them they all broke their necks to ensure that I had one. Two, I sat in the middle of the yard amidst them talking, drinking and smoking to get my write on. They didn't bother or wrangle with me to interact with them. They didn't call me weird, different or any other names that people usually use to describe me. They just let me be me. A lot of people say that I'm a mix between introvert and extrovert. I can agree with that. When I'm around my friends or family I'm just happy being around them. At these times I don't want to talk, play games or do anything but be there. They accept me for who I am and that is respected. I sometimes wonder if or how my success will change situations with my friends and family.

March 22nd

Aaaaaargh…everything is at a complete standstill. The book was supposed to be in print thirty minutes ago and the only thing holding me up is the book cover. I've sent text messages and called my friend several times with no response. I could be doing a million things but I can't do shit if the book is does not get sent off to print. Right now, I'm between depressed and worried. I don't feel like watching TV, talking to anyone or even writing but I have to keep my mind focused somehow. I know in a few months I'll look back at this and laugh but right now it feels like the world is closing on me and I'm starting to feel claustrophobic. I can't do anymore but just sit here. I hate being in this predicament. I know it's going to work out but damn.

March 23rd

"Just one of them days"… (Thanks Monica). I know I hit depression mode yesterday but today has been better. THE BOOK IS IN PRINT. Let me say that again. THE BOOK IS IN PRINT. Do you know what that means? That means on Friday (that's when I get the shipment of books) I will officially be an author. I will have designed my own suit. I had to pay an extra 100 dollars because it was a day late but it's all good. *Pause: Let me take the time to thank Debbie at 48 hours book publishing. She took a half hour out of her day to make sure that I uploaded the material correctly. Play:*

I am in the hole with money and have new bills coming in April but I now have a product. My uncle (Uncle Tony) gave me 100 dollars to help me push on to my dream. You know my best friend gave me 200 in the beginning of the month. I owe my barber 40 dollars. I still have to finish paying the web designer 15 dollars. My pops hit me with 50 dollars and I owe my home-girl (Jewell) who is making my cake gems 40 dollars. These are only some of the people who believe in my dream and now that I have a product I will show them what I can do. Of course they want to get paid but they believe in my dream to the point that they don't stress over the money. They believe that I have a real chance of completing exactly what I said I am going to complete.

To the kids: Accept encouragement with humility. Never get a "Big" head about your accomplishments. Stay on the path and stay humble. Being humble shows strength. Being humble shows respect. Being humble shows determination. Stay humble at all times.

I am constantly encouraged by other people but it's a full time job for me to stay humble. Being humble allows me to stay grounded. I remember a story I heard when a great king of the lands was afraid that he was getting bigger than he actually was. He hired a servant to walk behind him and when the crowd chanted his name he would have the servant whisper in his ear *you are only a man...you are only a man*. That is the constant voice that I hear in my head. That's how I stay humble. That is how I continuously connect with reality. My slogan is people helping people. I will always be here for the people. I will always stay grounded.

I had a good conversation with my friend today and we spoke on love. People really like to question me on the subject. I told him that I am truly in love with a past girlfriend. The love I have for her is the same love a married person has for the lost of their spouse. Even though I know I can never be with that person again the memory of her is what holds my heart in place. Even when I meet females they can't take the place of that special one. I like living my life this way. I think true love is when you feel nostalgic about a person. In fifteen years when I hear a song about a past love and I allow my brain to reminisce that means that person is forever emblazed in my mind. That's a form of true love to me. Since my love is still living I like to refer to her as the golden apple. Since the apple is a symbol of evil and the gold is a symbol of temptation then a golden apple is your sweet desire. You know that the apple is bad for you but the gold continues to tempt you. That's how I am with this female. I know she is bad for me but I am so tempted to touch. As long as I stay away I show strength which will allow me to continue on my path. If I touch it; I become weak. That is my dilemma. However, I choose to stay away but damn am I tempted. Welcome to the Raymond Goode show. I hope that you are enjoying my weird and wacky world.

March 24th

Today is the day of getting things in order. I'm two days away from the book signing and I'm still thinking of ways to make my table stand out better than everyone else's. I'm going to have a candy "bar." That's where people can grab a bag and fill it up with candy. *(I didn't know what it was so I thought I would explain it to you).* I'm going to have my newspaper clippings on the wall, I got the gem blow pops and I'm going to have a small banner. There is another author there and I wonder if she's going to the extreme like I am. I believe that all artists who believe in themselves should sell themselves.

I would like to take the time to give a shout out to all of my back pack rappers (or what I like to call backpackers) who helped me along this path. I would like to thank Atmosphere, Pharoahe Monche, J Dilla, Kidz in the Hall, Mos Def, Talib Kwali, Citizen Kane, Rhymefest, Hi-Tek, Souls of Mischief, The Procussions, Lyfe Jennings, D.J. Jazzy Jeff, Little Brother, Common, Blue Scholars, Solaa, Never Yet Contested, Blak Twang, Can-I-Bus, A+, Shyhiem, AZ, Dead Prez, The Foreign Exchange, Gym Class Heroes, Erykah Badu, and Skillz (Formerly Mad Skillz…represent V.A.). These are only a few of the artists that have put my mind in a relaxed mode when it was time for me to relax my mind. The ability to stay in the true form of hip hop is hard. The industry has ways of tearing an artist down and if you don't stand for something then you will fall for anything. Even though a lot of these rappers will never be main-stream I would personally like to thank you (backpackers) for continuously pushing the art that you love doing. There are people listening and supporting your efforts.

I remember when I first fell in love with hip-hop. It was Nas's 1st album entitled, "Illmatic." He had this song "It ain't hard to tell." It was the hottest song that I had ever heard at the time. I remember trying to memorize the lyrics and couldn't remember it no matter how many times I listened to it. I finally sat down with a pad and a pen and wrote down the lyrics.

"Streets disciple, I rock beats that's mega trifle

And groovy but smoother than moves by villanova

You're still a soldier; I'm like sly stone in cobra

Packin' like a rasta in the weed spot

Vocal's squeeze glocks, Mc's eavesdrop

Though they need not to sneak

My poetry's deep, I never fail

Nas's raps should be locked in a cell

It ain't hard to tell"

That's when I first fell in love with hip hop. To this day that is probably the only song that I can cite from beginning to end with no problems. I'm not saying that other artist didn't influence me; I'm just telling you when I fell in love.

2ND ENTRY

One day left and I will officially have my book. My occupation will officially turn to author. That is truly amazing. It feels funny when people say that I inspire them. Now people want to write their own books. Of course, I offered to assist them with fulfilling their dreams. One of the guys that I used to look up to back in the day (Robbie Walker) hit me up on facebook and told me that he was proud of me. I told him that meant a lot to me since I thought of him as one of the "cool guys from High School." He told me that I have the juice now *(Line from the movie Juice…Rest in Peace Tupac).* He told me that I was following my own destiny and that I should never stop. *Pause: Wow…reading those words really made me feel good. Play:*

Anyhow, I've been reminding my family and friends of the book signing coming up on Saturday. So far, everyone I talked to said they will show up Saturday to support me. It feels as though the entire city got my back. I think everyone believes in something bigger than themselves and they feel like if I make it then they do, as well. Let me tell you 1st…when I make it then every single one of you has made it. This is not just my dream but it is our dream collectively. Every one of your energies gives me energy. I always say that if I can make it then anyone else can make it as well. I'm from the gutters (Hillside Court) and I worked my ass off to get to where I am today. When I reflect on every situation, heartbreak, fight, awards I've received, book I've read, friend I've had or whatever it is I've been through…all of it has made me the man I am today.

I can proudly say that I am a positive black man. It takes a lot to say that but I can. The realization of the last line just hit me hard. I never viewed myself as the "positive black man" but I realize it now. It is a beautiful feeling when I can "see" it for myself.

To the kids: Strive to top your role model. Look at the traits that your role model has and fill those shoes. Analyze the steps that they take and not only duplicate them but find ways to improve. I pray that I am a role model to a lot of kids and I want to use myself as a road map for them to improve on. Analyze what I did to "make" it and see my flaws and come up with ways to improve them. I have made a lot of mistakes and that's what I want you to analyze and make better. I expect you to make it in a shorter time. I am only a man; I breathe the same air you do. I want every single one of you to be better than me. I will continue to raise the bar high because I expect you to rise above it.

Today, my barber (Jacob) said, "You putting a lot into this book." I told him that this book is my legacy. It's either this or I put a bullet in my brain. I'm past the suicidal stage now but that's how I intimately feel about my project. It's like gambling and when you're down to your last dollar. That means your back is against the wall. I want to feel as though if I don't make it then I'm out. I have to make it. There are a lot of people behind me. Thank you…thank you…thank you; I can't say it enough…THANK YOU. I won't let you down. I love you all in a place where there is no place or time (Thank you Donny Hathaway). I love you all.

March 25th

It is officially here. Today, I held a book with my name on it…MY name…yes; my name is on my book. I don't even know where to start. I first went around showing the book to people. *(I can't sell it because I want to have a good number of books for the signing).* Everyone is super impressed. My mother was the first one to buy a copy and I gave my grandmother a free copy. By the way she is doing very well. I am absolutely stumped for words right now…I am proud of myself.

March 26th

Today is the big day. Today is the official book signing party. I'm excited and eerily calm at the same time. I spent yesterday patting myself on the back and now it's time to go back to work. I have to pick up a few more trinkets for my table (rose petals, receipt book, bags for the candy bar etc…) so I can be fully prepared for tonight. Everyone is encouraging me and I like the fact that when my mom picked up the book she went straight to her story. I know that all the people I interviewed in my book will go straight to their story. I think…NO…I KNOW everyone will be 90% satisfied (at least I hope they will). I can imagine people reading their stories while they are sitting in their vehicles, bathrooms or at work. I can see them showing it off to their friends and family and saying "that's me." I vowed to get their stories out there and I gave up everything in order to do it. I may have experienced bumps and bruises along the way but I have fulfilled part of my destiny. Furthermore, I had to borrow fifty dollars so I could get an outfit for tonight. I went to Marshall's and saw a red and white polo shirt that I thought went perfect with the book but it was thirty five dollars. I was so tempted to purchase that shirt because it was perfect but costly. Then, something hit me. I have options. I decided to shop around and if I couldn't find what I wanted then I would come back and buy the polo shirt. I went to Burlington's, Ross Dress for Less, and finally to Macy's hoping to find something from the sales rack. I met this very energetic female who told me that I showed lots of enthusiasm about my book. She wanted to help me pick out my outfit. I told her that I was on a fifty dollar budget and she went to work. She found me two shirts and a pair of pants for forty seven dollars. She was so excited that she gave me twenty percent off everything to ensure that I could get the outfit.

To the Kids: *Explore your options. Sometimes your first option is too good to be true…shop around. My story is a metaphor for kids to know that you don't have to settle on the first thing you see. The world is huge and there is always more than one way to tackle a project. Or as my family says, "there is more than one* *way to skin a cat". If one school doesn't accept you...find another. If a rap label turns you down...keep looking. The world is full of so many people who are ready to say no but it is full of many more people who are ready to say yes. Seek and ye shall find...SEEK and ye SHALL find...think about it...Seek and ye shall find.*

I spent my last night playing cards with my cousin and niece, Nicole and Shanice. I spelled it right didn't I? (Inside joke) I know that after today my life will take off and I need my family to know that I will always be there for them. Even when they feel neglected I'm right there. My friends all think that if I make it then so will they. That is very true...I will take care of everyone. Not in the manner that they think but I have a master plan and they will see it as it unfolds. My family and friends are what made me and I want everyone to see the finish product. It is traces of them that make me.

March 28th

First of all let me apologize in advance for what I'm about to say. *Traces of You* is here. *Traces of You* is here. This has been a long and bumpy road but I've loved every minute of it. *Traces of You* will make writers put down their pens. I did my first book signing last night and I sold fifteen books. After people stopped coming to my table I went to them. I circulated the club so much that I was going to the same people twice. The other author left at 12:30am but I stayed until 4:30am. I couldn't stop. I went into a selling frenzy.

I woke up this morning in that same frenzy and drove all around town selling my book. I know it seems like my energy should be depleted but I still find time to write and its 1am. The support that I'm getting is tremendous. I think people see my drive. I met more dudes that bought my book than females. They want to support and I love it. I set up my table immaculately last night. I had a black and red tablecloth, my book (of course), key chains, business cards, cake gems (blow pops that are made of cake), candy bags, and ornaments. I even had red floating candles. I know some people thought my table was super feminine but I didn't give a fuck. I enjoyed the entire night.

I did have pros and cons though. Some drunken females sat at my table and were cursing and acting foolish. I could deal with all that but I saw one of the female's lean over and spit in my corner where I had my stuff. I told the security guard and he kicked them out of my section. Then, he brought over the security rope to ensure that the only people who came by were buyers. I loved that V.I.P status. I didn't have to use physical strength to handle the situation. Me and my entourage were called all types of bitches and hoe's but we didn't give a fuck as long as they moved. They talked about me like a dog every time they saw me but I handled it with style. The club was hood and I still sold well. I'm trying to bite my tongue when I speak of other authors but I'm gunning for everyone.

Back to business: I called everyone in my phone today and went from one side of town to the other and back to hustle. I heard all opinions and views on what people see in my cover. I made sure that they saw the price (ha-ha). When I looked at Omar Tyree's blogs; he said that he had to become an aggressive seller. You have to step out of your box in order to make a sale. I don't agree with the contents of a lot of his books but I will follow the key points to success. My publicist told me to go and look at other people's books to learn their techniques. *Pause: I think that's a good technique on one hand but personally I simply don't want to. I think that my style is good and I don't want anyone else's influences. I believe in learning from other people but I'm tired of learning. I have spent the last thirty two years learning and now I want to spend the next thirty two years teaching what I learned. I'm not saying that I can't learn from new people but I am saying I want to be a role model to others at this point. Play:*

There is a chink in my armor though. I dedicated my book to a very special female. Today I went to her parent's house and gave them the book. I battled with that decision. Wooooow…I'm stumped for words right now. That is the one that my heart belongs to but if I'm with her it makes my other goals drop. It is the memory of her that keeps me strong…not the presence. As long as I'm not with her I can continue on my path. If I'm with her then my brain pattern goes haywire. Sigh…the golden apple. Woooow… is that what true love is? When your brain pattern is interrupted? I am literally sitting back thinking about this. Damn. You won't catch me in this rare mode too often but I would like to give a personal dedication to Stevie Wonder's *You and I.* You (the world) have seen a lot of me tonight. I gave you a rare mode. You always see my spirit but I just gave you a piece of my soul. That's all you get…I'm done writing for tonight.

March 28th

Woooow…this has been such a busy day. I am literally on the floor outside of 105.7 fm (radio station) in Richmond, Va. This is actually the 1st time I've had a chance to sit and chill. I've covered so many parts of Richmond today that it's a damn shame, but I'm moving units. I talked to Mitch Malone (*the radio personality of 105.7*) and he told me to be here around 5:30pm. I got here at 8:15pm. I know what you're thinking (*I should have been there on time*) but it's so hard for me to pull away from people who are buying my book. I like it when they open up and begin to tell their stories. When people see ambition they want to open up to me. I enjoy talking and seeing people light up when they can express their past. Absolutely everyone has a story and absolutely everyone wants it to be told. I had to sneak in the radio station building by catching the door with my foot when someone walked out. I knew he (Mitch Malone) would be recording until 9:30pm so I'm prepared to sit until someone walks out. I got a pad and a pen so I'm good right now. This has been the first time today I've had a chance to relax. I sold 15-20 books today and I can't stop now. My friend let me rent his car for fifteen dollars a day. Damn it feels good to have friends to depend on. Everyone wants to know how to write a book and I tell them the same advice.

1. Start writing- Don't focus on your style and don't over think. Just start writing and enjoy.

2. Clear your mind- Stop focusing on the distractions in your life. Wife, kids, job, bills, etc. This is your time to focus on nothing but yourself.

3. Find your vice- Personally…a six pack, cigarettes, music and a blunt is my vice. It allows my brain to flow freely. Your vice may be different than mine. I'm not telling you to use my method but you have to find your own.

4. Be yourself- Don't try to be the "next." Don't try to be the next Jay-z, Omar Tyree, Tyler Perry, Kim Blunt, and Maya Angelou. Be the new you.

5. Research, Research, Research-I can't stress this enough...Research everything. (Example: let's say you're writing an autobiography and you are attempting to explain a restaurant that you were in. You have to remember how the glasses set on the table, pictures on the wall, what the woman at the next table was wearing, the music that was playing and even the color of your shoes that you were wearing). All of these points play a part in your writing process. You have to be thoroughly detailed without being overly detailed.

6. Writing is therapy- this should be number one. When you write it will give you a chance to relieve yourself. Remember to have fun. Your job is your job. Writing is refreshing...enjoy.

March 29th

Recap: The other night I met Mitch Malone from 105.7 as well as Sean Anthony from 92.1. I did a YouTube video with the both of them. They both seemed enthused about my project. It tugged at my brain if I should give them a book versus making them pay. That stumped me for a long time but I guess sometimes a few palms need to be greased...that's the nature of the game right? That night I was fatigued but I still found the energy to make it to a night spot and sell one more book. Any opportunity is an opportunity.

I woke up today determined to sell as usual. I went to Patient First and sold some books. I went to downtown Richmond and saw homeless people standing on the corner asking for money. I thought to myself *why not stand on the corner and sell books*. That's exactly what I did (ha-ha). I sold one book and actually did a documentary of it. That was great. I'm learning that I need to pack some snacks for when I'm out and about like; bananas, nuts, water or whatever. I hate spending my money at fast food places. The food makes me feel sluggish plus it's unhealthy.

Later tonight, I went to a soulful restaurant (Tropical Soul) and got on stage to sell my book. While I was waiting I needed to retrieve more audio c.d. books from the car. I ran into one of the guys that I did a story on in *Traces of You*. He said he had no money to buy the book but he wanted to read it. I stood there and let him read his story (*Even though I was passing up my turn to go on stage*). While he read his story I was nervously pacing back and forth across the floor. You see stepping on stage and talking to people does not scare me…it's what I'm designed to do. But standing there hoping that the story I wrote impressed him gave me more butterflies than anything else. When I heard him laugh at a particular part it made me feel good. He told me that I had pinpointed him. That was a magical moment for me. That's the reason why *Traces of You* is so important to me. Those moments right there.

March 30th

Damn my heart is racing. I sold out all 50 books. I had to give about five away but I was on my grind. The energy is super high right now. I shot my first commercial today. I got an actor and an actress and went to work. My boy (Stooby) is allowing me to rent his car for only fifteen dollars a day. He believes in my dream…he is a true blessing in the sky. From the books I sold I was able to re-up on money and I ordered another shipment of books (because I expect this weekend to be huge). I sold fifty books on a slow week when "people" did not have money. Imagine what I'm going to do when they get paid.

My brain is on fire with this directing stuff. Since my Youtube channel is like a television show I feel like it needs commercials. I plan to do commercials like crazy. I love commercials in real life. It is the only time you can see a beginning, middle, and end all in thirty seconds. I think that's the beauty of commercials.

The support that I'm seeing in Richmond is huge!!! It feels good when your city supports you. Let me tell the world (in support of Richmond) there is a lot of talent here. We are a mixture between up north and down south. You never know what you will get when you come here. One day we're listening to Master P and UGK and the next day we're rocking Wu-Tang or Common. We are home of the final four VCU Rams; Our Cinderella story. Don't get it twisted…them boys is playing their hearts out. I know that Wiz's "Black and Yellow" was written for the Pittsburgh Steelers but that song has given Richmond the energy that we need. I saw more than 3000 people jamming in the streets. The traffic was back to back.

Let me and VCU show the world what can come from this great city. Don't ever play us...we will surprise y'all.

I need to give a big up to some of the greats who inspired me along this path.

Malcolm X: Your teachings have shown me what is necessary to survive. I promise to never turn the other cheek. I will stand for all things that make me a man. If I need to stand with a shot-gun beside the front door in order to protect my family then I will. I will keep your teachings forever in my heart.

Martin Luther King Jr.: I promise to practice peace at all odds. I am learning how to live with my enemies. I understand why black and white kids should go to the same school and play at the same playgrounds. I see the importance of unity not just in the black community but in the world as a whole. I understand the words of "We shall overcome." I can't speak for the world but I promise to do my part to uphold the visions that you saw.

Isabella Baumfree (Sojourner Truth): For you I promise to never forget the struggle. I learned hardship from you. I learned what a strong black woman is and should be. I learned the very essence of the word woman from you. You have taught me that a woman is to be strong especially in her beliefs. You ran through swamps and back roads and even conquered the fear of the white man. You are a true inspiration to every black woman and man in this world. I will continue to live through the vision of you.

Michelle Obama: Good job...in my book...good job. You have and are embodying the meaning of the word woman. You are a combination of every strong woman that has come before you. You are making history. I am very proud of you for the person that you are. They say, *behind* every good man there is a good woman. Sorry...I don't believe that. I believe that *beside* every good man is a good woman. You represent the queen that I would like to have on my side one day. Continue to be you. I love you.

There are so many greats in this world that I could go on forever. I see all of your visions. I see what you all believe and fought for. I promise to do my part as a man to be a man true to my words. ROAD TO OPRAH.

Chapter 5

I can't worry about how the world will accept me; I can only worry about how I will accept myself.

April

April 4th

I'm in my calm before the storm mode. I re-upped on my books since I was all out on yesterday. I chilled at home, watched television, and cooked with my nieces and nephews. I needed a day off but today I'm back on my grind. My first commercial went very well. It feels good directing. I told you that I am an introvert/extrovert kind of person. I still get very shy in front of the camera. I continue to get on camera because I know what needs to be done to "make it" in this game but I'm mighty comfortable directing. I'm in downtown Richmond at this restaurant called the Urban Farmhouse waiting on my second interview with Vernal Coleman (reporter at Style Weekly free press). They were one of the first papers to interview me before I left so I will always give him a call whenever I touchdown.

To the Kids: Patient- bearing pains or trials calmly or without complaint. Learn how to show up to an interview at least fifteen minutes early. Learn how to wait in lines, learn how to wait your turn. Patience is very essential to whatever task you're attempting to complete. Take time to iron your clothes no matter the attire. Take time to brush your teeth, hair, etc. All of these actions take time and patience. But the end results make all the difference.

I have a lot of places to hit today. I need to improve the way I purchase my books. I will start ordering my books earlier in the week to ensure that I am ready to sell by the weekend. I sold around 45-48 books in my first three days. I think that's pretty damn good. Debbie at 48 hour books said that she was impressed.

April 3rd

It's 5am and I am ridiculously tired from this weekend. I received my first shipment of books last week and sold out in less than three days. I received my 2nd shipment on April 1st and it was sold out by April 2nd. Nonetheless, things are going very well and I haven't even left V.A. I'm hitting up malls, gas stations, and even standing on street corners. It doesn't seem like work because I'm meeting new people.

The manager at TGIF told me that I couldn't solicit in the establishment but by the time she caught me I had sold over 12 books and 8 audio c.d. books. One lady gave me a 50 dollar check and told me to continue on my path. People love to see a prominent black male doing something positive. I've received donations from people who don't want anything but to support. One lady donated five dollars and in return talked to me for 15 minutes about Jesus Christ. In the same day a friend of mine told me that I am spiritually lost. I tried to explain to her that my whole life I've tried to impress other people and I was lost and confused trying to complete that task. But when I focus on myself I feel at peace.

My mom told me that I should give some money to the church because it comes back in seven fold (or something like that). I don't disagree but the things that make Raymond Goode, Raymond Goode came from all elements of life. When I sat in the five Percenter classes I was taught how a black man should conduct themselves and treat their black women. I learned how to connect with the inner spirit by reading up on Buddhism. Do I know where I'm going to go when I die? I can't say, but I try to make the best of my time while I'm here on earth.

I show compassion to my fellow man/woman every chance I get. I believe in the teachings of my forefathers; as well as, the teaching from the homeless guy on the corner. I believe that I can learn from each and every individual that comes across my path. The one thing that I love about people is the ability to speak…it's free. People enjoy talking when someone is listening. I enjoy listening to people more than anything else and *Traces of You* gave me the chance to meet so many interesting people.

Someone asked me why I'm not in bookstores yet. I will be, but at the present time I am enjoying conversations with each and every new person I meet. I like going person to person and seeing their initial shock of "who is this crazy person running up on me and what is he selling." When they find out that it's a book and a book of substance then it really grabs their attention. A person who exemplifies knowledge survives better than the person standing on the corner selling drugs. People like to hear a person talk especially when they have something to say. Damnit I have something to say (ha-ha).

I went to Southpark Mall (Petersburg V.A.) and I saw females holding a book signing at the bookstore. I asked the owner about setting up a stand and selling my books in her establishment. She told me to leave a copy so they could view it and if they decided to give me a book signing they would get 50% of my sales. 50% of my sales??? I'm sorry...you didn't write 50% of my book so I can't possibly give you 50% of my sales. That store pushed me harder to sell my books.

I walked around Southpark mall and sold roughly fifteen books and 12 audio c.d. books. I looked at those females sitting at their table and after analyzing their books I can see why they aren't selling. I'm not trying to be a hater on anyone else's product but I like to read something with substance. I don't want to read about one night stands or he cheating on her with him. That's too cliché. My friend says that I'm too hard on other people's books. I'm sorry but if you put all your hard work in something and only produce shit then that's what I'm going to call it...shit. I'm not saying I'm better than anyone else but I will speak the truth. I understand that (you authors) this is your job and this is how you get paid, but what does your book do to help the community? I'm sorry if you feel like I'm cocky about myself or my art, but the truth is the truth.

I've always dreamed of being great at something...Talking shit and being able to back it up. I knew I wasn't going to be great at sports but now I have something...writing. I loved Mohammed Ali's style. He talked shit but was able to back it up. I think his style bought arrogance and a lot of enthusiasm to the ring. That's why I'm a Jay-z and Lil' Wayne fan. I plan to bring a level of excitement to the writing game. I told you I plan to make writer's put their pens down. To the Reader: The question you need to ask yourself is; "is he really that good?" Don't worry...I ask myself that question all the time. You're still reading aren't you?

April 3rd

I'm not going to even front...I am fucked up right now. I've been drinking and smoking all day. I sold out again. I thought I was going to spend the day chilling but even on a chill day I still sold six books. I spent the day at my grandma's house but I chilled Raymond Goode style. I pulled my computer out and went to work. I love being around family because they allow me to do my own thing. I felt the rush of getting on the Oprah show. I think the last official day for her show is May 28th. I planted a lot of seeds but I need them to grow. Everyone else think that I'm moving at the pace I should be but my personal goal is the Oprah show. I'm scared about not getting on. I will continue to do what I do. But I need to do more. Hold on…hold on…hold on. This is my story and here I can allow my brain to be scatterbrain. It is beautiful to be in my own world. The book is going great. I sold 100 books in less than a week. That is amazing to me. I need to order more books. I'm sorry…my brain is not here tonight. This is one of those nights for me.

April 5th

I'm on one of my slow days. I got my first sale on paypal today. Thank you, Dale. *Pause: He is one of the kids at the group home that I used to mentor at. I completely underestimated the fact that one of the kids from the group home would be interested in buying a book. Play:* That put a smile on my face. I went to the radio station again and gave my book to Community Clovia (Radio personality) who told me she would be starting a book club in two months and I would be a prospect. I don't want to wait two months because I believe the Oprah show ends on May 28th. I need to go crazy with the book sales **NOW.** My back is against the wall but I haven't started sweating yet. I just continue on my path because I know that things will work out accordingly. Whatever is supposed to happen will happen.

The commercial game is getting crazy as I prepare to shoot my 2nd one tomorrow. Like I said before I enjoy directing. I like using regular people because I feel that they will go all out because of their nervousness. My friend showed my commercial around to her friends and they all thought it was hilarious. She asked me if I always had these thoughts or were they brand new ideas to me. I told her that I always had "crazy" thoughts but now I didn't think that they were crazy and I started acting out on them. I told her that it is a thin line between insanity and genius. When I first started this mission everyone thought that I was insane but now they are starting to see the genius side of it all. I also told my friend that I did think I was crazy. Crazy to me means that I think differently than anyone else (Or a lot of other people). When you see the end results of my master plan you will see how everything worked itself out and how every step evolved into the next phase. The fun part of everything is that I'm showing it to you on my Youtube channel (GoodeRaymond).

People tell me that I can't be downing other people's books because it's their craft and how they make a living. I need to apologize to anyone I offend when I call your books shitty. I can't help how I feel and I expect other authors to get defensive. You should be upset but when you come back at me just ensure that your facts are in order because I believe in my book like no other. I had to open my brain cells and block out every single thing in this world to focus on my book. So if you're offended on some of the things I say then feel free to voice it. If your argument is valid enough then I promise to open my ears and listen. I'm sorry…let me switch gears because I don't want to come off like the angry black man (ha-ha).

I'm really excited about shooting my 2nd commercial tomorrow. I added a new element to this one. I got a singer to perform in it. I want to elevate on each new commercial that I do. I feel like I can "make it" on my own but I don't want to. I want Richmond to have a part in this. I want to show the world the talent that we have and I'm going to exploit it to the "Tee." This project is not worthy if I don't include my city in it. The commercial next week is going to be crazy. I plan to shoot one every week and add new elements to each one.

My friend Shaunda, text messaged me after watching my first commercial and it reads:

"I had to watch it again. You are quite talented…I am elated that you continue to persevere through your journey…I will always support you in whatever you do…unleash your thoughts and the world shall be your oyster…always be the star that you are…always love…Miss Davis".

Damn that is the kind of support that I need to continue on my path. I would like to thank all the support that I've received from all over. Each and every person has been a blessing in my life and has assisted in the evolution of making Raymond Goode involve into a man. When I did my interview with Vernal Coleman at Style Weekly; he asked me was I ready to give up my mission and get my old job back. HELLLLL NOOOO!!!!!! I'm in it till the death bell rings. I've been without a job for four months and I'm surviving well. I don't ever plan on clocking in at another job that I did not design for myself. I don't ever plan on working minimum wage making someone else rich when I have the ability to use my own brain. I'll stop when the heart stops beating in my body. I'm attacking this game at too many sides. This is only the tip of the iceberg…Keep watching and I will show you what my brain can accomplish.

I would like to give a special shout out the artist that kept me in trouble every time I listened to them: Tela, UGK, Scarface, Devin Da Dude, Three Six Mafia, T.I., Ludacris, Too Short, Goodie Mob, Outkast, Master P, Sillk Da Shocker, C-Murda, Snoop Dogg, Dr. Dre, Eminem, Xzibit, Warren G, Do or Die, Field Mob, Twista, Bone Thug, Ice Cube, Eazy E, Trick Daddy, 8ball and MJG.

Welcome to the Raymond Goode show.

April 6th

The 2nd commercial is done. I love using regular people but the new element (the singer) came through lovely. Martin Hall sung Carl Thomas's, "Summer Rain" beautifully. I knew he was the man for this commercial. Everyone I used today was super nervous about being on camera. That's a good thing. To me that feels like I'm putting V.A. on my back because I'm using regular people.

My cousin (Tayshone) just read his story. It made me feel good. I shot a documentary with him reading his story. You can check it out on my Youtube channel, GoodeRaymond.

2nd entry

Last year when I began writing *Traces of You* I had to go in total shutdown mode from the outside world. Even when I was at work; mentally I wasn't at work. I performed my job very well but that was all I did at work. I did very little conversing with my co-workers which in turn made people very judgmental and opinionated about me. Various sources told me that people called me arrogant, weird, different, asshole and cocky. It was even said that I was a devil worshipper amongst other things. The only thing I was not called was a child of God (ha-ha). I was the one of the most hated as well as the most interesting person there (Y.E.S Behavioral Health). I didn't let any of that bother me (*quite frankly I didn't care*) but I continued to be nonjudgmental towards anyone.

I contacted one of my old supervisors to inform him that I was going to attempt to contact a co-worker to be in a commercial. I knew she was one of the people, who negatively talked about me, but I like to focus on the good in people and I like to listen. I remember overhearing (she was talking to someone else) that her dream was to be a model and I thought I could help boost her career. Of course she didn't return my call and I guess I have to respect that. I just have to accept the fact that no matter how much I try to help people; some people just don't and won't like me. That's a tough realization.

To the Kids*: Remember these core values: Always be kind and treat others with respect and courtesy even when they are being disrespectful. It's called the, "Killing them with Kindness" technique. People will want to bring you down because they are ugly on the inside themselves. See the good in everyone because everyone has good inside themselves. It is your civic duty to help them pull back those ugly layers, so they can embrace who they truly are. You (yes...YOU) can be the driving force to change that individual.*

I will continue to be myself and see the good in every person. My friend (Soto) in-boxed me, after watching my commercial, and I would like to share that in-box with you because it meant a lot to me.

"I wish only the best for you. Keep working and you WILL get to where you want to get. You are one of the most strong-minded individuals that I've ever met in my life. I'm VERY proud of you Ray...Keep Grinding!!!!"

That meant a lot to me because every now and then, I need an extra boost in life. I work so hard that I don't ever get a chance to sit back and realize all of my accomplishments. I feel like I will get too comfortable and slow down. Before one project is over I'm already thinking of the next one. It's hard to believe that two years ago I was contemplating suicide and now I'm the ambition for people around me and afar. I figured out how to change the world but I had to start with the man in the mirror first (Thank you Michael Jackson). I am still an introvert person but that's how my light shines. I continue to work on myself and people see the glow and are attracted. That is the purpose of my journey. Slowing down is not an option because people are enjoying watching someone do the things that they only wish they could do.

I am elated (I just learned that word…ha-ha) to give people that dream. I pray that they follow my footsteps and follow their own dreams. People start getting old when they stop dreaming. WAKE UP PEOPLE. This is life…enjoy it to the fullest. Life is full of ups and downs but you have to thoroughly enjoy those ups and downs. Stop taking anti-depressant drugs and enjoy the depression stage as much as you enjoy the happy stages of life. When you emerge from whatever problems you are going through it will make you a stronger individual. There is no miracle drug out there; it has to be in you to change. Today…go outside and feel the breeze across your face. Look at the leaves rustling on the trees, look at the clouds moving slowly, stare at the stars, and listen to the birds chirping. Enjoy the beauty of life and what nature has to offer.

One of the quotes I used in *Traces of You* is "If the situation has not changed then you haven't changed". Go back to the mirror technique (Look in your eyes in the mirror) and ask yourself a question. "What am I doing with my life; what do I want to be in life; are my children/spouse proud of me; why do I hit my spouse; when I die, how will I be remembered; how can I change." These are some of the questions that need to be asked but the trick is to keep looking in your eyes and ask yourself these questions out loud. When you are able to answer your own questions without allowing your eyes to falter then you will start to see growth and maturity. When you can answer your own questions then you will be able to change your situation. I know it's going to feel weird but trust me…it works. President Barack Obama promotes change, even in the face of adversity. When your chips are down, you can still get back up. If you lost your job; get up. Lost a love one; get up. Incarcerated, homeless, finance problems…get up, get up, GET UP! I know that you can make a difference. Today is a new day in your book of life and I am your biggest fan. *I just stood on my feet and applauded your first step.* Now get somebody else to applaud for you as well.

April 7th

I'm sitting in the barbershop (Studio 3) waiting to get my haircut. I'm overhearing this conversation between two gentlemen sitting beside me. I heard one gentleman say "Speak it into existence, when you feel that you might fail then you have already failed." I chose to use this moment to teach since every situation can be turned into a teachable moment.

To the Kids: Speak your dreams and goals into existence. No matter what you choose to be in life…speak it into existence. Tell your friends, family and even strangers. Tell people that you are going to get an "A" on a test or that you will win a track race. Believing in yourself is the very first step in achieving. Your prior grade or last race does not determine the outcome of your next task. Only you determine what the future holds.

I will give you an example, even though, I really don't think you need one. Three months before I left for Chicago I started telling people that I was leaving. I received a lot of lukewarm responses like "yea that's cool, do your thing man" but they were said with doubt and disbelief. Two weeks prior to me leaving people started to realize that I was a man of my words and that's when they began to call me "Crazy" or "stupid" but people started taking notice of what I was saying. They started believing and listening to what I was saying. People couldn't process my brain thoughts and began to label and categorize me. I continued to speak my departure into existence. There was a small doubt of fear and I questioned if I was doing the right thing, but I am a man of my words and I couldn't back down. The day I left I stopped speaking it into existence and spoke it into existence.

2nd entry:

I'm in a rare mode right now. I'm feeling really good right now…I'm in my Daft Punk mode (Look them up…great band). I received some positive reviews on my book. A female (Kisha) called to tell me that my book is one of the greatest books that she's ever read. She said that she was a true novelist reader and she mainly read Christian and inspirational books but my book put her in a different mindset. She said that she only read nine chapters and she could not choose which story she liked better than the other. She asked me if I did research on my stories or did I just make up the details. Of course I did research on my stories. I told her to put me to the test and look up anything out of the book that she wanted to. She told me that she's never read a novel like mine.

My pops told me, "Don't ever let anyone take your dream away from you." In his own way he was telling me to stay focused. He also told me, "Make sure you get a house with a lot of acres so when you step outside to piss people living around you won't see you." That was his way of telling me to invest wisely. Pops is straightforward. There is no sugar coating with him at all. I guess you can see where I get traces of me from (ha-ha). I have to share the new text I received from Dale (remember he was my first online sale).

"So what's your next book gonna be titled?? The great one? Lol orrrrr you know what you should do is write a book for a younger age group such as like teens and write what you've been through and all that and how you became what you are now…

1. *"A great son*

2. *A great author and most importantly*

3. *A great big brotha and a father figure to me…you've helped changed my life from what you taught me."*

Wow…I actually touched one of the kids I had the pleasure of working with. That is quite possibly one of the greatest feelings in the world. I know I've helped kids but when someone communicates it to you then it makes a difference. My time in the social services field was not in vain. I made a difference.

I don't mean to turn this book into a shout-out book but there are so many artist that are worthy of praise. These dedications are to those soulful cats that always seem to come through for me every time I press play. D'angelo, Bilal, Anthony Hamilton, Floetry, Maxwell, Kem, Lauryn Hill, Dionne Farris, Raphael Saadiq, Raheem Devaughn, Erykah Badu, Jill Scott, Ledisi, Solange, Usher, Jean Grae. *Pause: Personal shouts out to Jean Grae. Google her right now and listen to her song "Love Song." I don't like to single out an artist, but I believe that she needs a boost. Send me some flowers girl and continue to do what you do. Play:* This on one of those nights I feel like I can write forever but I'm on the last page of my composition book.

Welcome to the Raymond Goode Show.

April 9th

The phrase of the day: "If you fail to prepare then prepare to fail." I didn't allow my brain to flow this week and didn't set up a book signing for Saturday night. I had one at the restaurant, *Bella Italia* last night that went extremely well. Richmond really showed out and showed love. But today I was slow rolling and didn't get out of the house "fully" until almost 5pm. I was caught in the super flea market soliciting my book. Every club I asked to do a book signing at turned me down. I knew I had started too late in the day to try and set something up but I guess It's just one of those days (thanks again Monica…hahahaha).

I found out something very interesting today…I went to two night spots (Satellite and Martini kitchen) and they are both owned by Asians. Both of them shut me down and I mean shut me down completely. They told me that I could never do anything in their establishments. That caught me off-guard. Most of the people that come through their establishments are black and that is how most of the clubs' money is made…from black people. But the one chance they get to help a black person they turn their backs…hmmm. I hate hearing no. I'm going to have to shut them down. I may not be able to set up a table and do a book signing but I will walk around their club selling my book. You won't turn me away that fast. If I can sell at least one book before I'm booted; I'll feel good.

You can't stop me…let me tell you the genius move that I received today. I saw a homeless guy today (Omar) asking for change. A great idea hit me from nowhere. Everybody who bought my book has given me rave reviews. I decided that I would give him my book and ten dollars. I told him to read as much of the book in three days and when I return I would give him another ten dollars for his honest opinion on *Traces of You*.

I stand behind my project. I want somebody who does not feel as though he has to be opinionated because he bought the book from me. I want him to tell me the pros and cons of the book at no cost to him. I wanted to see what he would say without being pressured. *(I thought this was a really cool idea)*. I can't wait to see what he says about it.

I ran into a snag today that really made me think about the privacy act. I guess the people I interviewed for *Traces of You* didn't actually think I was going to write a book. First and foremost, I understand that when I interviewed each person they confidentially told me their answers and I would never want to jeopardize people's lifestyles; however, I did inform them of the reason (writing a book *Traces of You*) as to why I was interviewing them. Well, one of the characters became upset that I told his friend's mother that one of the stories was on him and his relationship. I have to respect people's decision to not want to be known. *(I'm learning this as I go)*.

People shared their inner most feelings with me and even though some don't want people to know of their "inner personality" they are still proud that I took the time to write about them. Sometimes I can't hold my excitement about my project so I unintentionally selfishly hurt others by not thinking of their feelings. I can be a selfish prick and sometimes I don't know what it is I've done wrong until someone brings it to my attention and I would especially like to thank Brandon for bringing this to my attention. I will promise to uphold the privacy act of each and every person in *Traces of You*. I feel as if someone confides in me their most inner feelings then I will do my part to keep it confidential. *Pause: I'm glad I was able to get that out of my system because that really bothered me. Play:*

It's around 3:30 am on April 10th and since I haven't been to sleep yet I am still calling this entry April 9th. I am sitting in IHOP writing and I have my books on the table. People are seeing my determination and are coming to me about my book. The most interesting part so far is that I met two white workers at IHOP who seem to be very interested in getting the book. At first the white female waitress told me the same answer that every other white person gave me... "Come back next week and I will get your book." Then, she began to read the back of the book and became impressed. She instantly reached in her pocket and pulled out the fifteen dollars for the book. I told her she was the first white person to buy my book. Then, I asked for her permission to use her name in my book and soooo...Erica Coleman...this is your shout out in my second book. Thank You for supporting me and *Traces of You*.

So, you're probably wondering why I'm so excited...well, when I went to Short Pump mall people looked at me and acted as though I was the scum of the earth. I'm really trying to refrain from using the "N" word but that's how they looked at me. It wasn't just the white people but it was the black people, too. So, I personally would like to thank Erica for her contribution.

The night started off bad since I was drinking and it seemed like I couldn't get my mojo at all. Every place I went kept turning me down and I couldn't seem to sell a book to save my life. Then, I decided to return to the Martini Kitchen and get my hustle on. I went to work in that place. I knew I couldn't bring my satchel in the establishment but I also knew they wouldn't say anything if I carried two books in there at a time. *Pause: I thought that was pretty smart. Sometimes I impress myself. Once I set out to work, I go to work. Plus, I had to put my mind to it because my aura was fucked up earlier tonight. Play:* So, when I went to the Martini Kitchen I had the sole plan of chilling and refueling to get back on my grind for Sunday. However, things began to happen once I let my brain settle. People began inquiring about the book and before you know it I was in the full swing of things. I clearly understand what it means when people say, "you have to spend money in order to make money." I had to spend ten dollars to eat but I got to use their table with the chance of speaking to people around me.

I'm enjoying life right now. My job is to sit in restaurants, lounges; café's, bars and sell books. While I'm chilling I'm continuously writing for my next book. This is quite possible the best job in the world. This is also where my introvert/extrovert style comes into play. For example: I'm sitting here with my books on the table, I have my crazy haircut, and I'm writing in this composition notepad sitting at this table alone at four in the morning. Everything about me screams *Look at me* but I am so comfortable in my own world and wish to not be disturbed. I know all of this sounds weird but when I'm zoning, I completely black out everything around me and focus on nothing but myself. Sometimes I just need a break from the world and I mean the entire world. With the exception of me getting my books out...I am totally zoning and you know what...I need a break from this pad and pen as well...peace out. Welcome to the Raymond Goode show!!!!

April 10th

It's officially April 10th. Now that I was able to get some sleep I made my way to the super flea market. My goal is to at least sell two books which will cover the twenty dollar charge for renting a table, as well as double my profit. I never plan to sell out but rather to sell one book at a time. I try not to have any expectations when I start selling (*I have a lot of hopes though*).

I've been getting rave reviews on my Youtube video of Omar. I hope that he really gets his life together. I wish the best for everyone and I pray that he gets his life in order so he can move forward and progress. I wish the same for each and every individual. As people get older life should get easier. People should continuously work on progression. Life becomes hard when you stop moving. I try to keep moving and encourage people around me to continue to move. I spoke to this woman yesterday who told me that me being able to step in so many people shoes and detail their lives was "scary." I knew that my book had a sociological side to it but I never took the time to realize how deep it delved.

April 11th

Good day, good day, and good day. My people really showed up today for the filming of my third commercial. I would like to Thank Chris and Kesha's family for bringing a different element to the commercial. *Pause: I chose a multiracial family to show real life family in America. I thought it was a good move. Play:* Terrell Thank You for showing up and out on every project that I do. Last but not least, I would like to give big-ups to Mish (Coakley) for doing a stand out job in the commercial. She really got into the part of being a police officer evident by her wearing the police shirt/badge/holster and hat. She killed the game when she showed up with the 45 automatic Beebe gun. She told me that she was a professional and she proved it today. If you haven't seen the commercial then you need to check it out. *Pause: You can go to GoodeRaymond's YouTube channel. Play:*

My initial plan for the commercial was for Terrell to get hit, but never to fall (because I practice safety first). However, he volunteered to take a hit and I mean a hard one. He put a smile on my face. He did his thing. *Pause: I am very proud of everyone who continuously assists me on my journey.*

My camera man, Marquis is one of the glues that have held this project together. Thank You. We are getting to know each other enough that he is starting to give me feedback on what is going on. In the beginning, I told him I couldn't pay a lot of money for one commercial, but I could pay a little money for a lot of commercials (ha-ha). I have to give credit where credit is due and it is surely due to Marquis. Personally, I believe the best time to thank a person is during my book because I'm zoning in on them, what occurred that day, and why I'm so grateful for them.

Overall, today was a really good day. I woke up this morning and emailed channel 12, channel 6 and channel 8 news stations. I also sent emails to all of the individuals I received business cards from over the weekend. I went to the bank to inquire about opening a business account. I visited John Marshall high school and saw some of the old teachers that I used to work with. This visit sparked an interest within me to do motivational speaking. *Pause: Woooow…please don't let anyone put me on their stage and talk (ha-ha). Play:*

On this busy day, I managed to also visit a Christian restaurant called "It must be Heaven." *Pause: I enjoy eating in locally owned business because I like to put my money back in the community. Play:* I showed them my book and they instantly flipped to my acknowledgement page. They glanced over my "Thank You's" and focused on the line that read, "God, Allah and Buddha." Appalled, the woman slid her hand down the page and showed it to her friend. Then, the owner began to preach to me about how Allah and Buddha were false idols and that I was wrong for my beliefs.

I proceeded to explain how different religions helped me to become the man that I am today but she proceeded to say, "Ain't no way possible that a fat man sitting down can be a God." I thought that was highly offensive. Even if you don't believe another person's religion it is not right to disrespect it. Let alone to completely disregard the black man standing in front of you trying to do something positive. I saw the comment as being completely unprofessional. I completely understand the criticism that I will receive from the world regarding by views but I believe people should focus on and respect the fact that I am a black man doing something positive. If that's too straightforward then I'll go back to my childhood days where the saying goes, "*If you ain't got nothing nice to say then don't say anything at all. Pause: World...please be respectful and kind to each other. Play:*

I practice individuality and try to be respectful of everyone no matter how different they are. This is what needs to be done on a universal level. I read a quote by W.E.B Dubois when he spoke on double consciousness. It reads:

"*Double Consciousness is the sense of always looking at one's self through the eyes of others, of measuring one's soul by the tape of a world that looks on in amused contempt and pity.*"

I'm not good at being or trying to be someone I'm not. I only try to be me. I know who I am and I'm proud of whom I am becoming.

April 12th

Today, I went to my publisher's house (Kim Blunt) to go over the next steps to moving forward. Back to work.

April 14th

After so many people told me that I needed a promotional package; my publicist and I put one together in a matter of hours (six to be exact). It came out really good. So, I went back to the radio station to give Sean Anthony one of my packets. I told him that I was doing everything that I'm supposed to do to the fullest of my potential. I told him that I'm walking the walk and going down the path that I'm destined for and now it's time for help. Now it's time for other people to have their hands in this project. He told me that he liked my hustle and that he would assist me in any way he could because he loved seeing black people doing something positive.

Since all the radio stations are in the same vicinity, I went to 92.1 to provide them with one of my promotional packages. I spoke with Big Keith from 92.1and he informed me that I spoke well and he would keep me in mind.

Sigh of relief. Everything is moving in the manner that it's supposed to move in. I'm not expecting anything to happen overnight. I am enjoying the fruits of the struggle. I hope now they are taking me a little more seriously now.

Pause: I would like to thank a good personal friend of mine, Jewell. She is a very special person to me. She has held me down on a lot of my projects and has been that encouraging voice in my head when it was needed. She will make a great wife to someone and I'm sorry that I can't be that one. Play:

On this road to, wherever the hell I'm going, I'm going to experience a lot of heartbreaks but I have to remain focused.

To the Kids: *The definition of Focus is the main emphasis; concentrated effort or attention on a particular thing. When you're focused there are a lot of things that will attempt to hinder your process. Some things are not intentional but intentional or not you may still veer off of your course. Remember to stay focused and keep your goals in sight. The worst pain is not finding out that you veered off track but rather that you never got back on track. People have hardships in life and end up grasping at the threads of life simply holding on instead of refocusing and getting back on track. Once you get focused you will acquire tunnel vision. That is when you will be able to see the finish line.*

To be quite honest *(I'm not trying to be harsh but the truth is the truth)*, most of the females that are in my life are everything that I want BUT nothing I need. I'm looking for the one that is EVERYTHING that I NEED. Will I ever find that kind of love? I don't know. I can only focus on one thing at a time. I am completely head over heels in love. I am actually married to this pad and pen. I think I told you this before, but Raymond Goode is dead. What you are seeing is a dream...my dream.

Moving on...OH YEAH. I called Bridgette today (you know...from Chicago). I re-thanked her for her assistance and informed her that my book is alive and well. She was very impressed and said that she would buy one from my website.

April 15th

Woooow…you ever had one of those days that it just feels good to wake up (that should be everyday right…ha-ha). Today is just one of those days to sit outside and chill. Randomly, I reminisce on a time when my cousin (Will) from New York had asked my cousin (who sell drugs) what he had been up to. Here's the dialogue:

Will: What's up, what you been up to?

J: Nothing much still hustling getting it in but I'm looking for a job

Will: Don't you sell drugs?

J: Yea

Will: Well if you sell drugs then that should be your full time job.

I thought that conversation was particularly funny. I left my jobs to become an author. This is my full time job. When people ask what my occupation is I tell them I'm an author. It feels good to say that. I'm not depending on unemployment or a job to eat. I'm completely on my own and using my God-given talents to take care of myself. It feels good to fly on my own.

2nd entry

I sent my book and my marketing plan to the Barnes and Nobles Corporation in New York. I have my fingers crossed and patiently waiting on their response. I also went searching and think I found a new printing company. Basically, I'll be getting more books for less money. Now, I'm just waiting for them to send the proof of *Traces of You* so I can make sure it's up to my standards. The proof is supposed to be in by Tuesday. *Pause: Next week's my birthday and I had almost forgotten it but I think I want to throw a "Traces of You" party but it would be no use if I don't have any books. So I'm pressing really hard to ensure that I have them. Play:* I think things are moving along as they are supposed to move. I'm impatient but I'm not rushing.

I chose a great business partner (Thanks, B) who is comfortable with doing all of my behind-the-scenes work. As long as I hold down my part of the deal (stay hustling), then I believe we are going to make a great team.

I learned something today. I submitted my own write up to the local newspaper "The Voice." Marlene, the editor, informed me that my story was not in paragraph form and most editors would not have bothered to even read it (*she actually said she was getting cross-eyed from reading it*). Then, she stated she would put it in paragraph form for me. I'm glad she told me that, because now I know that I have to let my partner proofread my material before I send it out to any companies. I know what I want to say but I don't know how to put it in corporate terms. I'm glad she relayed that valuable piece of information to me. Now, I'm wiser and that's a problem I can fix.

I'm getting closer to my dreams. I saw Oprah's website today and saw that her show is ending on May 25th. That will be a very sad day for me and not because I may not make it on the show but rather because I will have to end this book and move on to the next book project. This book has served as my own personal diary. I expose things about myself that most people would choose not to show the rest of the world. I've given every emotion whether it was up, down, angry, happy, cocky, scared, frustrated or whatever else you chose to see when you read *Road to Oprah*. I got the same feeling of sadness that I felt when *Traces of You* was complete but life is about progression and at the end of the day, I must move forward. *Pause: I'm talking like the book is ending tonight huh? (ha-ha) Play*: I just want you to see how dear each book is to me and the emotions that I go through regarding one of my books coming to an end.

To the Kids: *Learn how to let go. Learn how to let go of that boyfriend/girlfriend, that altercation, that bad grade, those problems at home. Growing up is learning how to release and let go. Letting go gives you the opportunity to move on to the next stage of life. Letting go is not a bad thing; it shows signs of maturity. On this Road to Oprah I have learned to let go of a lot of things no matter how painful there were. I have met so many young people who* *refuse to let go of a past love no matter how bad the relationship was…LET GO. I met so many young people who gravitate towards the street life and hold on for dear life because they are afraid of progression…LET GO. I've seen young people killed over a petty argument because they cannot let go…LET GO AND GROW. These are some of the reasons why so many of our young people are sitting behind bars and don't fully understand why they are behind bars until they are behind bars. I encourage so many people to let go and live life to the fullest.*

April 15th

I'm sitting here watching a new author (Edward Burt) type several memoirs on his life. Feels good to see a new artist put his work in the game. I'm guiding him through this process. I'm trying to show him the ropes while I'm still in grind mode. I pray that this is the level that I will always stay at. Nothing is more beautiful than seeing another artist at their best. I want to conduct seminars on how-to-write and expand your brain in order to put together your best work. Anybody who asks me how to write a book, I want to be able to give them the same knowledge that I was given and now have. That is my promise…to always help people from my level down and never up. As I said before my slogan is People Helping People. To me the meaning of life is to be able to help your fellow brother or sister. It feels good to do for yourself but when you've acquired all or some of the knowledge from life then you should spread it. I tell people that I spent thirty two years learning and I will spend the next thirty two years teaching what I've learned. Every situation that I've been in is a teachable moment.

Sorry…the boy is feeling good right now. I've had a few drinks and smoking so I'm in chill mode right now. Lil Wayne's, "I'm Single" is playing right now and as you all know that is a chill mode song no matter what the situation is.

I find it funny that every word I put down will be viewed by the rest of the world. At this point I can write something funny, educational, serious or crazy and people will read it. I always write *Welcome to the Raymond Goode show* and I truly mean it. *Road to Oprah* is phenomenal. I like the quote from one of Biggie Small's songs that state, "Stereotypes of a Black man misunderstood." That is a very powerful line.

My mind is sporadic. Once an idea clicks inside my brain, I go crazy with it. I find ways to tackle that problem or idea. It's the same as when I was in Chicago and was turned down from Social Services. My brain snapped to ways to fix the problem. I learned from working with kids that there is no one solution to fixing a problem. There are many solutions to fixing a problem. And this brings me back to motivational speaking…I'm so ready. I'm ready to stand in front of a crowd and tell people my ideas on the world. I'm ready to unleash what I know to the world. I talked to a friend that wants me to come to Lynchburg in order to speak to the college there.

I also talked to my business partner who told me that she knows the ropes to get in contact with local colleges, prisons, alternate schools etc. I'm glad that I have someone in my corner that allows me to continue to move forward with my artistic views. I may not know the words that need to be said but I know what I want to say. I'm glad that she has the ability to say it for the corporate world. I like to know that I hold my full reservation of words for my interviews. I know that I've put together a good team.

To the Kids: *See your friends for the abilities that they possess. Each and every one of you are completely different from the person beside you. Every one of you has completely different traits, hobbies, skills etc. Ask them for help and offer your services to them when needed. "People helping people" is my motto and most people don't mind extending their services to help a friend.*

April 16th

I spent last night helping my niece start to write her book. I started typing up my brother's book entitled, "All the Above" and I'm guiding my friend through his book, "A King's Heart." Everyone has a story to tell and I'm honored to be the one to help them get their stories out there. From the outside looking in, it seems as though I should be stressed with so much on my plate but I stay eerily calm. I like helping people and that is what I'm designed to do. I feel as though everyone has the talent to express themselves. I'm glad I am able to inspire people around me to express themselves through writing which I believe is so easy. It only requires clearing your mind to be able to freely express yourself as I mentioned in my earlier posts.

My brother's book is going to be good. I informed him of the steps that needed to be taken to allow his book to come to past. I told him that I would charge the bare minimum and this only included the costs for what is needed to get the book in print. No extra expenses. He told me that he trusted me and hearing that felt good. I have to throw 100% strength behind his project because well…because he's my brother.

My friend Bear wants me to write the prologue for his book. I'm not a fan of writing for someone else's project because I only hope that my words will match what they want said. But all I can do is put my best foot forward and hope it's well received. This is my job (ha-ha). My job is to inspire people…damn I have a good job.

Me and my brother are so different but yet the same. If it wasn't for him I wouldn't be in the position that I'm in now. Long story short, my brother was one of the biggest drug dealers on the block and had the type of "mafia" team that once you got in, there was no getting out. I told him one time that I wanted to sell drugs and he fronted me a pack. I walked halfway down the street and a police car came zooming my way so fast that it looked like it was coming straight for me. My knees buckled and I didn't know whether to run or keep walking. The police car sped past me and I turned around and went back to my brother's house. I gave him the pack back and told him that this life wasn't for me. He said "cool" and took it back. He has never pressured me into doing anything I didn't want to do and kept me away from the street life by not letting me hang with him. That gave me the opportunity to explore my own life and make my own decisions. That is why I will put my ALL behind every move that he decides to make.

My niece is very defiant and does not want to write but at the age of thirteen she has already lived a full life and is a very exceptional writer. She is rebellious against the world but I know that she has it in her to be anything that she wants to be.

***To the Parents**: You have to stay on top of your kids. Show interest in their work. It requires more than asking them how their day was or how was class. It*

*requires you sitting at the table with them as they are doing their school
assignments. Even if you (the parent) know nothing about the subject that they are
working on; still sit with them and give them attention. If the child is struggling to
clean their room you have to go in the room with them, pull out a chair, turn on
some music and talk to them while they work. Kids need attention. Kids need
attention. Let me say that again like Beetle-Juice: Kids need attention. If their
attention needs are not met at home then they will find it in other places such as;
girlfriends, boyfriends, streets, drugs, gangs or whatever vice they find that will
give them that attention. I beg and plead that each and every one of you parents,
uncles, aunts and grandparents play a large part in your kids' lives because we are
losing too many of them to the graveyards and prisons. I know a lot of people can
tell you what the problems in America are but they can't tell you the solution. I
have given you two very simple steps that can be done to help fix the problem. The
only time you fail is when you don't try to fix the problem.*

I'm heading back to the radio station this week. I'm excited because when I
return I will have a copy of my write up in Richmond's *Style Weekly* and *The
Voice* plus my new commercial on YouTube. I'm expecting this new commercial
to go viral. I truly believe that this is going to be the one that puts me over the top.
I'm getting my plans together to release *Road to Oprah*. The same excitement I felt
for *Traces of You* (that it is the greatest book in the world) is the same feeling I
have for the book that you are currently holding in your hands. All the time, I tell
people that as many times as companies tell me "No" that's how many times I will
keep coming back. All "No" means to me is that I have to go back to the drawing
board to derive a new plan on how I will come back stronger each and every time I
walk through the doors.

2nd entry

I think everyone looks at me like I'm superman. I have to tell you that I am
like everyone else. I still get scared over stuff. I get depressed (severely depressed)
and lonely at times. Sometimes, people observe me and think that my heart is cold.
They tell me I act like I can single-handedly hold the world on my shoulders.
Honestly, it feels like I can sometimes but I still have weaknesses (even when I
don't show it). The only time I feel empowered is when I write. My words are a
representation of me. It is how I overcome my fear. When I do my interviews the

strongest points is when I am talking about my book. That's because I know I poured my heart into it.

It has finally hit me; the world is ready to embrace *Traces of You* and I'm ready to move on to the next project. Everyone tells me to focus on the sale of *Traces of You* but that is getting old to me. I don't care what the world thinks about me; I only care about how I view myself and my personal goals. My old publisher told me to focus on selling my first book because I wouldn't want to have two books on the shelves not selling. Sorry…they're going to sell. It has to sell because my heart is involved.

I worked all day typing and editing *"All the Above"* and I was in dire need of a drink. The feeling kept growing and growing. So, about one o'clock in the morning I decided to go to the Bella Italia (restaurant) to get a drink. No notebook, no computer, I wasn't even wearing my *Traces of You* coat. I just wanted to chill. I began talking to the bartender (*T-Pain I'm in love with the bartender*). She showed me love and gave me a free drink. Then the D.J. came over and bought me a shot. Then, the bartender gave me another drink. This was all for free. *Pause: This was all cool because I really didn't want to spend the money. Play:* This is the type of things that happen to me all the time. This is one of the reasons why I know that I will be successful. I just have to be patient and enjoy the ride. I think most artist forget how to enjoy the ride and get to the top too fast. I'm enjoying the setbacks that I encounter. I'm enjoying every "No" that I receive because it makes the "Yes" so much sweeter. *Pause: Is it bad that alcohol and weed frees my mind to write? Ludacris said, "Whatever gets your juices flowing weed or speed." I guess I found what gets my juices flowing. Play:*

April 18th

Ohhhhhhh yea…. I officially opened my business account today which is a major step on this road. I'm looking into finding an accountant when this project really starts taking off. I liked the woman (Monique) at the bank who seemed like she wanted to be apart of my team and was really confident about her accounting skills. She saw the business opportunity in my project. I'm letting my business partner handle that portion of it. I want to be involved as less as possible because I want to be able to completely focus on my craft. I'm wild and crazy and know how to get in the front door of places. I know what it takes to be the front-man. That's all I want to focus on. It's where I flourish well.

I'm really excited about going back to the radio station this week. I've been showing my commercial to everyone I encounter. Monique (the banker) said my commercial was innovative. I didn't know what that word meant so I had to look it up.

Innovative: Featuring new methods; advanced and original

Damn…when I looked the word up it put me in a different mind frame…Innovative.

Funny story: My partner saw me buy a beer, raised her eyebrow and stated, "You are going to mess up your career before it even gets started well." My sister and I were joking about what she said. My sister said, "She doesn't know that's when your brain is at its best." This is absolutely true. I'm not saying that I'm getting drunk out of my mind but drinking and smoking does unlock creative parts of my brain.

April 19th

Today is a good day. I received a phone call from G and G magazine who wants to do a story on me. They are a Christian company who believe in my dream. She told me that she would give me two full pages. So, that's free advertising for me; I'm in. I ran it thru my publicist to make sure she knew the ends and outs.

Furthermore, I just saw part 2 of my write up in *Style Weekly* newspaper. I feel like I'm on my Goapele's "Closer to my Dream" mode. People are starting to take notice and I have another write up in Richmond's *The Voice,* which will be coming out tomorrow.

April 22nd

Today is one day before my b-day and things are continuously looking up. Everyone loves my write-ups in the newspapers and the "Police" commercial has skyrocketed to 121 views in less than two days. My new strategy is to hit all newspapers and free presses in the U.S. I started looking up different newspapers in different states which will give me more exposure. It doesn't matter if I'm from V.A. a positive message is a positive message and I need to utilize all sources that can push my message further.

Community Clovia from Power 92.1 radio station finally hit me back and said that she wanted to speak to me further about my book. I'm excited. Things are going according to how they are supposed to go.

I spent the other day emailing different newspaper companies and I immediately got a response from a newspaper company called *D.C. Spotlight* in Washington D.C. I sent them a copy of my book as well as my marketing plan. *D.C. Spotlight* said that since I was trying to involve Oprah they wanted to quickly review what I have so they can assist me in publicizing my book.

Then, *Urbanviews weekly,* a local newspaper, told me that they wanted to do a story on me. I know that all I need is one link to connect me to another link and right about now I'm starting to connect the dots. I am going 1000 beats a minute. Once this door is cracked I'm going to kick it wide open. I have so many ideas running through my head and I have to try each and every one of them. I won't stop at books and movies. I have inventions that I want to try my hand at. My friend called me abnormal. Now you know I had to look that word up.

Abnormal: Deviating from what is normal or usual, not typical.

My friend said that most people my age usually have kids and sometimes grandkids. I tip my hat to anyone who have kids or grandkids at my age and are enjoying life but that is not the path for me (at least not yet). It's too hard focusing on me let alone someone else in my life (ha-ha).

I'm starting to get criticism on *Traces of You* but the overall response is that it's a great book. I'm ready for the criticism but at the end of the day, I really don't care. This book is my gateway. This book opens the door to endless possibilities and I plan to explore each and every one of them. I am going to enjoy life to the fullest and let the world take care of the world.

April 23rd

It's 3am and it's MY BIRTHDAY. It feels good just to be alive. It feels good to have focus in my life. Now, I have a lot under my belt. It's been a good year so far. I know people always say, "This year is going to be my year" but this year is really going to be my year. Everything is flowing too smoothly right now. I don't ever get a chance to recap my achievements but when I let my brain relax I must admit that I'm proud of myself. I keep reading the articles written in various newspapers on me, over and over again. My book is gracing people's book shelves and book clubs. People are taking me seriously. I have critics…actual critics. That means that they read my book first in order to critique it. It feels good to know that I have a legacy, something with my name on it. It feels good to have found my place in this world. I found my niche and I'm sorry for anyone that has not found theirs. It feels good to know that I have a place in this world. I've been in this game for four months and I'm moving at leaps and bounds. I would like to give a personal shout-out to Richmond, VA. People always told me that in order to "make" it; I would have to leave Richmond, VA. I'm proving them wrong as Richmond continues to show me love.

April 24th

I'm still recuperating from yesterday. I spent the b-day with my family enjoying myself. *Pause: As I'm writing Chrisette Michelle's "Epiphany" is playing. Thanks Chrisette. Play:* I went running tonight. Like I told you before…that's when I clear my brain for new ideas. Initially I couldn't come up with a new idea to top my last commercial but it came out of nowhere. Now, I'm going to spoof commercials. Damn that's a genius move. My friend told me that I'm pushing a book like a rap c.d. The game is about to get disgusting.

My publicist told me that I need structure. I hate that word. I do better being wild and free. You know what's really cool. I'm not even trying to get "on." I don't care if I ever "make it," I'm just doing what I love and having fun doing it. I can't worry about how the world will accept me I only worry about how I will accept myself.

It's four months in the year and I'm moving at record speed. Is it crazy that this whole process seems easy to me. All I have to do is be myself and let the world be the world. The world will catch up to me. I remember Puff Daddy saying in the Biggie movie, "Don't chase the money; chase the dream". That's exactly what I'm chasing. Money is too easy to make. To me; it's only a piece of paper. I'm looking for so much more.

I looked up my horoscope on Taurus's. It said that we are patient, reliable, warmhearted, loving, persistent and determined. Those last two words stuck out to me. I am a very persistent and determined kind of person. I know what I am worth. I have a brain and I'm determined to use it. My mind is what I want people to respect about me and not the fact that I'm cute, strong, crazy, witty or stupid but the fact that I use my brain. I want people to respect the fact that I'm not afraid to be me. That is my true angle to break into this game. I'm not afraid. I'm not afraid of what the future will bring.

Let me switch this as Lil Wayne plays. Is it crazy that I want this life? I understand the females that will come. I understand the shady people that I will encounter. I understand how the media will try to downplay me. I understand the monster that I will become but I can't stop it. I just pray that I will continue to be the person that I am right now. This is what I call core values. I know people will say that I've changed but I am still the same person that I am today. I still like being by myself. I like working out, I love writing, I love being me. I love being me. I'm going to say that again, I love being me. I love the simple things in life such as: The way the wind feels when it hits my face; the way good music makes me feel; the way I raise my left arm for no apparent reason; and the way I feel more comfortable and free when I'm by myself than around people.

Right now, I'm getting lost in my own thoughts as I listen to this real jazzy song by J. Rawls entitled, So Fly. Check it out and get lost in your thoughts for a little while. I want to continue to love listening to artist live. I want to continue to enjoy having conversations with my mother. I want the simple things in life. It's the simple things that are my core values. These are the things that hold value to me. These are the things that will keep me centered.

I talked to an ex-girl (Kia) today. She asked me who the feminist female was since she knew it wasn't her. She wanted to know who had struck a chord in me so deep. It felt weird telling her that side of the story but the truth is the truth. She asked me the usual question about if I was still with her and if not did I still talk to her? I wrote in my *Traces of You* dedication that the book would be my last love letter. I stick with that but fuck it I'm zoning right now:

Nicole,

I hope that you are watching the progress that I'm making. You asked me a long time ago if I thought I was the man that I thought I should be. I can finally say yes...I have reached man status. I am becoming the positive Black man that is needed. I'm trying my best to stay as true to myself as I can. I dropped a book off at your dad's house. He seemed very excited to be holding it. Please don't think that this is some cheap ploy to get you back but if it was it would be genius (ha-ha). I always told you that a lot of things that I do may start off being about you but it would end up being for me. You started the "Traces of You" project but I will take it through leaps and bounds. Continue on with your success and I am truly proud that a strong black woman is succeeding. Continue to succeed and I will always be a true fan. I'm proud of you even though I'm not with you. Forever in your presence.

April 26th

I started brainstorming on quite possibly one of the greatest commercials ever. I plan to spoof all the commercials that are already out there. Being a genius does not mean that I have to come up with new ideas but rather capitalize on the genius ideas that are already out there. I know that this commercial will be something that the world has not seen before. Damn, I'm ready to show the world that I can do this. This commercial (Snicker's spoof commercial) will show my creativity. It's scary and fun at the same time because it's new territories that I'm treading. I know it's going to be good because I'm doing something that I love.

I have a makeup artist who is willing to go the distance to ensure that I will look the part. My home-girl, Angel told me that I continuously surround myself with good people that constantly want to help me. My mom said that I have God's favor on my life. I suppose they are all right. It feels good to know that people are energetic about something. I feel energy when I include new people in my projects. At times I feel sluggish with what I'm doing but I feed off of other people's energy. I really hope the world sees the contribution that I'm making for it. I'm giving people that extra spark that they need to smile. As long as I remain positive then I truly believe that I can change the world. My mom always told me that I can't save everybody but I will give it my best shot. I believe that everyone has a dream. Absolutely every single person out there and I want to be that person that can help them achieve it. Maybe I can't save the world but I will give it my whole heart.

I think that was the dream of my forefathers and ancestors. Give your all to the world no matter the consequences, no matter the backlash. I want to give my all to the world and pray that I make a difference in somebody's life. Even if I can't save the world I know I can save one person. They say it takes a community to raise a child. I'm a part of that "community" now. This book, *Road to Oprah* is so important to me. This book will be a constant reminder of the person that I truly am. I don't want to get lost in the "worldly" way of things. This book will constantly remind me of the things that are pure in life. This is the book that I will read to keep me grounded or as some would say…grassrootish. Stereotypes of the black man misunderstood (Thanks Biggie).

To the Kids:

Reminisce: Indulge in enjoyable recollection of past events.

Remember to allow your brain to reflect on the things that make you smile; whether it is a person, spiritual guidance, a place or event that you experienced. It is vital to keep those things close to your heart. They say that you will never know where you are going unless you know where you came from.

April 28th

I meant to write yesterday but I was in a slump mood until my shipment of books came in. Even though I'm not worthless I feel as though when I don't have my product in hand, I am. Of course, once those books came in, I went to work. I knew it was Wednesday (two days before payday) so it was going to be a slow selling day. I went to Chesterfield Towne Center (where I was previously kicked out of) and sold three books. It's only when I get in selling mode that the blood in my body goes 1000 beats a minute. After the mall, I went to TGIF (another establishment where I was previously kicked out of) and once again I was met with the same demise (ha-ha). They can't stop me though. Every time I have books I will continue to hit these places up.

I ended up talking to this guy who said that my mission of getting on the Oprah show was impossible. I will give you his exact words:

"Brother: I'm a businessman and realist. Trying to get on the Oprah show is impossible plus you shouldn't be out on the streets running around selling books. You need to have a team doing this and I can help you."

I'm sorry brother your first mistake is saying that anything is impossible. If that was the case then Martin Luther King Jr. wouldn't have made all the accomplishments that he did. President Obama would have given up a long time ago. All hell, G.I. Jane would have given up. He gave me his business card and told me to call him. I'm not saying that he can't help me but when the first sentence out of his mouth includes the word impossible then we have no reason to talk. I will use the word impossible on May 25th when the show goes off the air. Until then the dream goes on.

CHAPTER 6

If God has put favors on my life then I willingly open myself and will go in any direction that I'm directed to go in.

MAY

May 1st

In another twenty four days the Oprah show will be over. I might not make it but my dream is still strong. Can't stop, won't stop. I am hearing more and more negative feedback on my "Road to Oprah" mission but I keep my wits end upbeat. I stay open and optimistic. I know the rest of the shows are already scheduled but I have to stay strong. I have to push on.

Today, I managed to get kicked out of Southpark mall in Petersburg, Va.

I also went to Newport News today. I know I can sell books in my own city but I continuously test myself. I have to know that I can sell in other cities and states. I think I sold pretty well today until I got caught and kicked out of the mall there. But once my brain settled and focused I went into work mode. I found every hair store, barbershop and beauty salon that there was and went to work. I stood outside of Costco in the parking lot and sold books. I couldn't stop. I sold ten books and five audio c.d. books.

I met a Hurricane Katrina survivor today. She told me about the struggles that she went through in New Orleans. She told me that life was better for her in Virginia. I gave her a book and an audio c.d. book. I felt like she deserved it. I don't care about the money that I lost over the book I just felt like she was deserving of something and I gave her what I could. I pray that something I can do for somebody else can bring some sort of excitement into their lives. There are so many things that are bigger than money.

Last night I shot a Youtube video where I gave a shout out to all my backpackers. A backpacker is someone who knows how to "make it." They are the people who carry their marketing plan, cds, movies, books, pens, pencils, paper and whatever else they think they need. Backpackers are always prepared and optimistic about the future because you never know who you may run into when the time is right. It feels good to call myself a backpacker. It feels good to know that I am in the fight like everybody else.

Honestly, I feel like I have a better chance than anyone else. People compare me to Tyler Perry but let me tell you now…I'm no Tyler Perry. I can't say what his mind went through before he stepped into the game but when I left

December 31st and I have been screaming that I'm going to be a star. I can't say what his vision was and I'm not trying to "diss" him but I'm saying that my style is different from his. This is my vision and my plan. My commercials are mine. My words are mine. My videos are mine. Raymond Goode is the name that will be on your lips. I'm going to do things differently. I'm going to do things my way. I'm going to break boundaries in leaps and bounds.

You know what…sometimes I scare myself. Sometimes I let my brain relax and listen to the words that I say. This is one of those times. Everything I wrote so far makes sense. Every word that I've written has touched you whether different or indifferent, but you continue to read even though you know I'm crazy (ha-ha).

I really want to give Tyler Perry his props. *You are a black man doing something positive and I will give you your props on your endeavors.* I would also like to give respect to Will Smith. *You two have given the game a new element. Both of you have given the generations to come something great to look up to and I tip my hat to the both of you. I only wish to follow in your footsteps. To the both of you: I promise to be the strong positive black man that is needed. Even when I don't agree with your opinions I will continue to be that strong force that is needed in this world. I don't know if I can do it in the way that you two have done it in but I will do it in the Raymond Goode way. I just want to give you two your props in advance.* This is one of those nights that I don't want to take the pen off the paper. I am feeling good tonight. I ended the night the way I wanted to end it. I'm sitting outside with a pad and a pen. It is 4am and I have to hit the road in five hours. I have to end this…Welcome to the Raymond Goode show.

May 5th

Atlanta today; Chicago next week, 250 copies of *Traces of You* sold, 150 audio c.d. books gone. I am definitely moving units. In less than 25 days the Oprah show will be off the network and this book will be complete. This "Road to Oprah" has definitely been adventurous and I am truly enjoying the struggle. It feels good to support myself. My job will allow me to see the world on my own. My job is beautiful. I get to meet and converse with people from all walks of life. I like the fact that people open up to me when they meet me. People enjoy meeting someone that is doing something positive and they offer their assistance whether that is a donation, buying a book or audio c.d. book, or offering words of encouragement. I accept anything positive that comes my way with humility.

I explain to people that I am only selling a book; Plain and simple. No matter how you look at it that's all it is. People are buying into a dream. It is my dream but it is a dream that we all share. Everyone (and I mean everyone) knows that they have a lot to offer to this world but the restraints of "life" hold them back. Mental death is the king of all terrors. When you are mentally dead then life stops moving and you become mentally old. I love the phrase "Wake Up" by Spike Lee. To me, this means you have to break the chains of life that binds you and begin to grow. Stop seeing the world for how ugly it is and see it for the beauty within it. Behind every dark cloud is a silver lining. Your brain is the dark cloud and silver lining. You just have to learn to appreciate the darkness as well as the light. You have to recognize that when you are going through the storm there will be brighter days. If you can't appreciate the storm then there is no way that you will be able to appreciate the light.

May 8th

ATL bound, baby. Today I came up with the perfect plan. It's time to hit the world at full speed. It's time to run as fast as I can go. Next week I'm going back to Chicago. I've gone as far as I can go in Virginia. I have a product and I'm ready to give my all to Chi city. I've sold 225 books in less than a month. I'm giving light back to the reading game. If I can do this much in Virginia how much can I do in Chicago? I don't know if you can tell how excited I am right now, but I'm so excited. *Road to Oprah* will be out soon. Well, it's already out if you're reading this (ha-ha). *Road to Oprah* will now be the new words on your lips.

Let's switch for a minute. Lately; everywhere I go I've been seeing images and pictures of Marilyn Monroe. Since I'm a writer I am observant of things like this so let me introduce you to Marilyn Monroe:

"Born Norma Jeane Mortenson in 1926. Marilyn Monroe combined equal parts of sex and glamour to capture the American fascination with stars like few

before or since. Although not an author, much of her childhood was spent in orphanages and foster homes. This loneliness and subsequent hunger for attention and affection fueled her drive to stardom. Monroe's first movie role was a telephone operator in the Shocking Miss Pilgrim, Dangerous Years, Green Grass of Wyoming and You were meant for me. She had hit movies including; 7 Year Itch, How to Marry a Millionaire, Gentleman prefer Blondes and Some like it Hot for which she received a Golden Globe award for. Monroe was ranked 6th greatest all time female star of all time by the American Film Institute. Monroe was crowned the "Miss California Artichoke Queen" at the artichoke festival in Castroville. Monroe was an idol until her tragic and controversial death in 1962."

For the last three weeks her name continuously pops up in conversations I have with others. It's only appropriate that I introduce her to others and give her, her props. Good job Marilyn Monroe. Somehow you have struck a chord in my head. You are definitely an icon in the eyes that don't normally look at you in that light.

Ok let's get back to swag 101: Atlanta is wide open. Atlanta is jumping…Chicago is jumping and I'm ready to jump in all of it. I sold 225 books in less than a month in Virginia alone. What is the world going to do when I get in the fast lane? I saw what I can do in my own state and I'm coming at the world at a fast pace. I won't stop. I've heard over and over that *Road to Oprah* will pave the way for *Traces of You* and I believe it now. *Road to Oprah* will show the world that I am…DIFFERENT. *Road to Oprah* will totally surprise the reader that I can write a book like *Traces of You.*

Traces of You is my baby. *Traces of You* is my first born. I used to read a lot of books by other authors but now the only book I read is *"Traces of You."* I believe in it. After every single story I wrote I became super excited because I had the opportunity to view a snippet of each and every one of the interviewees' lives. *Traces of You* has means so much to me and I promised each and every one of the people in my book that I would push their stories to the fullest. I have made fifty promises and I intend to uphold all of them. It doesn't matter what the outlandish means that I have to go thru to fulfill those promises but I will go through them. I will live in self storage units, walk the streets day and night because I made a promise to fifty people and I will keep these promises.

I still can't get over the fact that I sold 225 books in less than a month. You must admit, I'm doing a pretty good job. As I previously stated, each one of you fifty people deserve to have your story told and heard by others. I'm fulfilling my promise to make that happen.

At this time, I would like to give a BIG shout-out to my niece who graduated from TNT Academy. *Takeysha, your uncle is SUPER proud of you. I've seen you grow into the strong black woman that you are becoming. I tip my hat to you and will always be there for you…*

Goodnight world.

May 11th

Today is the day. I'm sitting in Greyhound bus station getting ready to board the bus. The last couple of days my emotions have been running hard. I went through the fear stage, nervous stage and empowerment stage. But now I feel refreshed. I feel new. All the problems in V.A. are in V.A. Now, I chase new problems in Chicago. I'm ready to attack. This is the mode that I want to be in. Take no prisoners. Everyone has to buy a book. *Traces of You* is coming to Chicago quickly.

The bus has started moving making everything officially official. Goapele's *Closer to my Dreams* is playing through my headphones and I am on an all natural high right now. I'm looking at people around me and I reminisce when I used to sit in airport terminals and people watch. I used to write down what people were wearing such as; accessories, headgear etc. I would write about how they walked and their mannerisms. I don't know why I used to do that but I always found people interesting. Maybe that's why I believe in *Traces of You* so much. I had to analyze people's movements and actions in order to bring them to life. I think those times that I spent people watching really helped me with bringing my characters to life.

Let me share something else with you. Before I left my three jobs and went homeless I researched first time authors and why they are often rejected. I want to share with you how I responded to the questions that I found on Creative Solutions.

The market is too small.

Traces of You covers all people; Black, White, Puerto Rican, Asian, gay, straight etc. *Traces of You* covers all age ranges from 15-62.

It doesn't fit our list.

Traces of You fit's everyone's list because it describes people, delves in different languages and allows the reader to learn about people that they have never met before or places they have never been before. The music in the stories will be nostalgic as it ranges from Beethoven, Lil Wayne, Trick Grenade, Bob Marley etc.

This type of book doesn't sell.

I don't think a book of this magnitude has ever been put on the market. This book allows people to read stories about other people. I think that will always sell. The reader can visualize any one they want in place of the character.

It's not right for us.

Trust me…its right for you.

It's too narrowly focused.

Fifty people will give you fifty different perspectives on life.

It's already been done before.

It's never been done. I like to think about the movie "Ghost" when Patrick Swayze's spirit entered Whoopi Goldberg's body. I allowed fifty different personalities to enter my body.

It is an article not a book.

It is more than both. It is the blueprint to the blueprint. It contains fifty different plays, monologues, scripts, acts, scenes etc.

There's too much competition.

Tell me who they are.

It's too costly to produce.

The profit that you will receive from publishing my book will be substantial. The book is only a book but the man is so much more amazing.

You're not an expert in your field.

I am an expert at life and people. I study and listen to people which is my first nature. My second is piecing people together to form *Traces of You*.

This is the stuff that I wrote before I embarked on the mission that I am on. I went back and forth over leaving everything behind and chasing this dream. The pros outweighed the cons. I did not have the option to not go for this dream. I answered those questions as honestly as I could. I couldn't see anything holding me back.

In addition, I'm starting to get reviews on my Snickers spoof commercial. I knew that commercial would get me compared to Tyler Perry's, Madea. I in no way meant to copy him but as I said before I don't have to be a genius because I came up with the idea; I only need to capitalize on the genius ideas already floating around. I mean that in the utmost respect to Tyler Perry. I think that you are an amazing, strong black man who has stood on your own two feet amidst the world. I want to make it perfectly clear that I respect you in the utmost manner because I know how the media tries to switch things around and put brothers against brothers. But all in all it was a very good commercial and I'm very proud of it and of every actor/actress who came out to assist.

Back to Road to Oprah: We stopped in Maryland and I got off the bus to smoke. This guy told me that since he was a Bengals fan he liked the way the designs in my hair looked. He asked me if I wanted a beer. "Damn right I want a beer," I told him. Mac is his name; "Like Big Mac," he told me. I showed him my book and commercials. Instantly, the police commercial had him laughing. He said that he would definitely watch the commercials so I could get the "hits" on YouTube. These are the type of situations that happen to me.

May 12th

Somebody told me that I remind them of a verse in Nicki Minaj's song, *Moment for Life* when Drake says, "Everybody dies but not everybody lives." As I sit on the bus I realize that I don't know what's going to happen in Chicago but I'm going at it full steam. I like the scene in the movie A Knight's Tale when the guy was talking about why Heath Ledger was a great knight; he stated, "He never takes his eyes off his opponents." When I look in the mirror and ask who my opponents are; all I see is me staring back. I'm my only opponent. I am the only stopping force in my life. That's bad for the world. If I'm the only person that can stop me then there's nothing out there that can hold me back…Oprah bound.

May 13th

I woke up this morning feeling refreshed. I'm in Chicago once again and on the prowl. I found out today that the final Oprah taping takes place on the 17th. I only have a few more days to get on and I'm staying open-minded. I can't help but feel doubt and sadness about the possibility of not getting on the show, but I do know that it has been a hell of a ride. I'm selling pretty decent here. I sold about seven books and five audio c.d. books. *Pause: As I'm writing this I can't help feel a little bit down about having to end this book. I realize everything that has a beginning has to have an end. Play:* I stopped at the Malcolm X school which was very interesting. I saw the car that Malcolm rode in. I talked to a guy who said that he might be able to get me a ticket to the Oprah show.

2nd Entry

I spoke to this homeless guy for thirty minutes who told me all the problems that he's having in his life. It makes me want to kick myself for crying about the problems that I have (i.e.; like not getting on the Oprah show and not being picked up for an article). It felt good talking to him because those stories always snap me back to the realities of life. I am proud of the accomplishments that I have achieved and even though I may not get on the show I know that I've helped make a difference in someone's life whether it is through my journey, inspirational words or simply by laughing at my commercials. I've met so many cool people along the way. I've experienced ups and downs; walked the streets for hours, and been in situations that I wouldn't want to place my worst enemy in.

To Chicago: Thank you for giving me focus and direction. Thank you for giving me tunnel vision to complete Road to Oprah. Thank you for being the rich cultured people that you all are. Even when I leave this city I promise that this city will always hold a special place in my heart. Oprah...I am not done. Neither the dream nor the journey will cease. My mission is to meet you and I plan to complete that mission. You are a strong black woman that has managed to stay to your roots even amidst success. It is admirable of you to open a school to the impoverished in Africa and I greatly respect and honor you for that. Thank you for being that inspirational role model that you are and that the world looks up to. I will always be a fan of the Oprah Winfrey show but more importantly I will always be a fan of Oprah Winfrey, the person.

To the Kids: Never stop dreaming. It is the one thing that is your own. It's what's needed to survive in this crazy world. It is the one thing that keeps us alive as people. Embrace your dreams and you will embrace life. The sky is not the limit but only the beginning. Find your voice and follow your path. Remain an individual. Be kind to others. Treat people the way you want to be treated. If you believe, you can achieve. Respect your elders...even when they are wrong. Remember, one day you will be in their shoes. Turn defeat into victory. Build confidence and destroy fear. Master a formula and learn a new one. Power without heart and strategy is meaningless. You can't love anyone fully unless you love yourself to the fullest. Practice core values. Close your eyes and learn to walk in faith. Believe in something bigger than you. Strength embodies endurance. If the situation has not changed then you haven't changed. Find a role model and strive to top that person. The love of money is the root of evil. Challenge everything. Love and believe in yourself. Make your own goals and break them. If the world doesn't understand you, chuck the deuces to it and continue to shine. I love each and every one of you. Take a bow because I'm applauding you.

3rd entry

Oooooh Noooo...I've done it. Chicago I've kept it gully. I've walked the meanest and most dangerous streets where the gangsters and killers are supposed to be at. Real recognize real. I showed respect to every person that I came into contact with. I stayed in a self storage unit to fulfill my dream. These are the moments that I will never get back.

May 14th

I woke up running super late this morning. I was supposed to be at the super flea market at 6am but didn't wake up until 6:30am. I've gotten lost too many times to even count but I know something's going to work out when I get there. I'm kind of hungry but I can't eat until I make a sale. That keeps me hungry (ha-ha). I'm riding on Emmett Till Street and I felt the need to give credit to his story.

Emmett Till was killed August 28th 1955 for allegedly flirting with a white woman. Two white males arrived at Emmett's uncle house, took him to a barn and gouged one of his eyes out. They shot him in the head (allegedly), tied a seventy pound gin fan with barbwire around his neck and threw him in the Tallahatchie River. Till's mother transported her son back to Chicago where she held an open casket funeral for the world to see the injustice that the south had done to her son.

Whenever I think of this story I feel Emmett Till's pain. I feel the fear he felt when dragged out of the house desperately clinging to any piece of furniture that he could get his hands on. I can hear Emmett's grandparents begging for the white men to stop. I can see the white men throwing him on the back of the truck as they yell obscenities at him and drive towards the barn. I can see the white man holding a gun or weapon to Emmett's head and yelling words along the lines of, "Oh so you think you can speak to our women…well we are going to show you up north niggers how we deal with our nigger problems down here in the south.." I can see and feel the pain as they took turns punching 14 year old Emmett until their arms were sore and all while continuously drinking. I can see those white men urinating on Emmett attempting to fill his mouth, nose and open wounds. I can see those men throwing his limp body in the Tallahatchie River. I understand why his mother wanted an open casket funeral for the world to see what hatred for a race had done to her son. I would especially like to give an "all respect due" to Emmett Till's uncle, when asked if he had seen the culprits, he stood up in the courtroom of an all white jury, pointed to the two white men, and said, "Dar He." Those two words echo in my head and he is an iconic figure in my eyesight. I only hope that my strength embodies the courage that he shown.

2nd Entry

Today, I went to the "swamp-o-rama," the Flea Market, I got lost three times and it took me more than two hours to get there. When it was over and I was leaving it started to rain hard. I talked to this older gentleman who said he would give me a ride. As I got in the car I saw him putting a picture of Emmett Till in the backseat. *Pause: World, this is the type of things that happen to me. The type of things I observe and take notice of. Play:* We struck up a conversation and he told me that Emmett Till was his cousin and every chance he got he was buying pictures or whatever he could find of him. As we continued to converse, I think he was impressed by the extensive knowledge that I have of Emmett Till. I told him that I would shout his name out in my book soooo…Lavon Kelly or "Doc" as his friends calls him from Mississippi; I hope you made it to Wisconsin to play your game of golf. Oh by the way, I know that your kids and grandkids appreciate all that you are doing for them. I agree with you that Emmett Till's murder was a huge factor in the civil rights movement and I am saddened that it took the death of a 14 year old boy for that to come to light. His death was not in vain so I stand to my feet and applaud Emmett Till's life, the courage of his uncle, and the strength of his mother.

There is a lot more that I can write about tonight but I think it would be appropriate to end the night with Emmett Till's story.

May 15th

So, I've managed to make it to church this morning. I was sitting on the bus not knowing what church I should go to and a female got on with her daughter. I was instantly drawn and struck up a conversation with her. I told her that I was looking for a church and since she was on her way I would just tag along with her. She asked me why I attend church. I told her that I enjoy hearing the word. In general, I enjoy hearing people speak especially when they know what they are speaking about. Plus, I need the reinforcement of a good word from time to time.

The church I attended is, "Empowerment Temple" with Pastor Bobby Butts and Evangelist Dorla Butts. The young female's name is Alecia. She says that she is aspiring to be an actress but she does not know how to break into the acting world. I just hope that life does not get a hold of her because she is an energetic and outgoing person. Her aspirations are the same as all others. People know that they are here on earth for greatness even if they do not know what that greatness is. People are aware that they have a purpose in life but are afraid of pursuing that purpose.

2nd Entry

I've survived and I am surviving Chicago. I've let my persistence do it. V.A. stand up. You needed someone to rally behind and I'm here. My second trip is more relaxed, I'm enjoying my surroundings, and all that Chicago has to offer. First of all, let me give props to Derrick Rose and the Chicago Bulls. In this first game, Chicago got off on Miami. Rose, I see the Michael Jordan heart in you but I still believe that Miami is going to hold it down.

Oprah's last taping is this Tuesday the 17th. The only fitting way to end this book is to stand outside of the coliseum. I don't know what's going to happen but I'm ready to give it my all.

I saw this guy walking in the self storage unit with his book bag and I wondered if he was living the same way I was. It really hurts my soul that I will have to expose the storage unit. It is one of the things that I dread about this journey. I must open a homeless shelter in Chicago because it will be my fault that people in my situation will be exposed. People always tell me that I have a heart of stone and I have an "I-Don't-Care" attitude but these are the things that I should care about. I should not care about the selfless things that a lot of people care about. I care about the livelihoods that I'm affecting. You ask me why I'm exposing the self storage unit if I'm this hard against it. The storage unit is a part of the Chicago experience and I would not be doing my job to the world if I didn't report my experiences.

May 16th

Right now Bob Marley's "Three Little Birds" is playing. I needed something to calm my nerves. I didn't pay my storage unit this month and I am locked out. I tried to pay and the female had a nasty attitude with me and told me to come back in the morning to talk to the manager. She either didn't want to reset my code or I think that I've been caught. Either way this is very bad because the last Oprah taping is in the morning and I have to be there…ready. I don't mind jumping the security fence around the self storage unit but my problem is the security code on the door…aaaargh. This is not the time for this; All of this after such a good day.

The good day began with me visiting both the Chicago Defender and the Austin Voice newspaper. They both seemed very interested in doing a story on me. Afterwards, I sold some books on North Avenue and barely scraped up enough money to pay my cell phone bill. *Pause: I can't let this operation crumble over 60 damn dollars but you know me…when there is one problem there is always ten ways to solve it. Nothing is impossible but this is going to be a tough one. I have an idea but if I get caught on this one then I'm going to jail but I have to try it. Play:*

2nd entry

AAAAArgh…I waited until another vehicle showed up and snuck into the gates of the self-storage unit. I waited until someone used their security code and made it through the door. I thought I had escaped it all until I saw that they had put a 2nd lock on my unit. That caught me off guard so I guess I'm forced to sleep in the gym and figure out if I'm caught in the morning. I told my mom that I didn't care if I was caught but I would need my books. The clothes are just clothes but my books are a different story. I know I have to make it through this week at least. Fuck that…I'm going to make it through this month. *Pause: Just now I had the thought that I should get a job. I'm looking around and seeing all these people working to make someone else rich; People who are afraid to step out of their boundaries. I stepped out already and there is no going back for me. What I'm doing needs to be done. My problems are my problems and as I always say "For every one problem there are at least ten solutions." Play:*

To the Kids: *This life will throw you as many curveballs as it can to slow down your progress. You must know when a curve ball is thrown, understand the* *purpose of a curveball, and have your bat ready to hit the curve ball out of the ball park so you can return back to progressing. When life hits you hard it is your duty to stumble but not fall. It's easy to regain balance when you stumble but hard to get footing when you fall. This is called endurance. Endure the tough times that will take a toll on your mental.*

*   **To the World**: Listen up…Every time you push me I'm going to push back harder. Every door, every no and every discouraging word that is directed towards me fuels my anger. It makes me more and more determined. You are the reason why I don't sleep. You are the reason why my brain is continuously working. You are the reason why my commercials will only get better and better. You are the reason why I wake up in the middle of the night grabbing my pad and pen. You want to know where my strength comes from…well it comes from you world. You will give me the energy to make it. You want to know how to stop me…STOP SAYING NO!!!*

3rd entry

Okay Okay Okay…I had to work-out and work-out hard. I think my insides have calmed down. There were some extraordinary events that occurred today. I spoke to this woman on the train that really wanted a book but did not have the money to get one. She listened to my story and thought it was amazing. I joked with her about the crackers in her bag and told her that I was hungry. She told me that there wasn't any more crackers in the bag and instantly started digging in her pocketbook. She said, "I have 98 cents. Do you want it?" I replied, "Heck yea I want that 98 cents." It almost brought a tear to my eye. I appreciate that 98 cents more than any of the money I have received because I know it came from the heart. That was a true blessing. She dug deeper in her bag and gave me an apple which I ate on the spot. Thank you to that lady on the green bus line. It is your compassion that strengthens me.

At the Austin Voice newspaper company, I was given a pack of graham crackers and a sweet tea. That's all I had to eat but that's all I need when I'm working.

Alecia (female I met yesterday) asked me when I will stop trying. I told her, "I'm living in a self storage unit…I will never stop. I don't know how to stop." It's not in my nature to stop. I don't want this to sound weird but I'm enjoying the struggle. Every job I've ever had, I had to hustle to get to the top. I mean I literally broke my back to get to the top. My hard work paid off with me getting the Sr. Recreational position at my old group home in less than three months. I enjoy the hard parts of a job. Once people make it to the top things become more political and less creative. *Pause: I have a dilemma about when I'm going to end my book since the final taping of the Oprah show ends tomorrow. I have decided that I will end this book when I officially leave Chicago. I need to find a hole to sleep in now so goodnight world and welcome to the Raymond Goode show. Play:*

May 17th

I slept at the gym and got caught by one of the staffers. My physical and mental is literally running off of three hours of sleep. I'm back on the streets though. I rode the bus just to get some more sleep. I'm just not in the mood to do much of anything today. I understand what a homeless person goes through on a day to day basis. I am constantly defending myself when approached. I act as though I don't know that I'm in the wrong when I know that I am. I could easily throw in the towel and go home but there are so many homeless people that do not have that option. If they don't have that option then I don't have that option.

2nd entry

So the scare is over. I just had to pay my bill at the storage unit and everything is back to normal.

To the Kids: When your outlook on life begins to change it will become evident to those around you. People will notice change taking effect. You will not need to change your friends for new ones because sometimes those new ones are just the old ones disguised. You have to fully accept your change in order to be friends with anyone. Once your change process is completed, your old friends will be drawn to you because of your light and you will also attract new ones. The friends that shy away from your light were never friends...these kinds of people are called, associates.

May 18th

I'm sitting in the cafeteria at DePaul's admission building. I'm selling my books but I don't want to get caught by security so I have to scope out the area. I have chosen to talk to people getting on the elevators, therefore, I have to strategically time when I walk towards the elevators so that it's the same time other people are getting on the elevator. If I talk to them on the elevators I am out of the view of security; plus people generally won't call security if they say "No" on the elevator.

I came to DePaul with no money and I managed to sell two books. It wasn't me selling but more of my hunger for food selling my books. I had absolutely no money on me and I was starving. I know I had to do something. I started talking to everyone and managed to make twenty five dollars in less than ten minutes. Even though I'm hungry I can't waste money on fast food. I have to spend it wisely. My nerves are settling because now I have a few dollars in my pocket and two people have my book. I am trying to grace the entire city with *Traces of You*.

Once again, I am meeting some of the friendliest people in the world right here in Chicago. When people don't have the full amount for a book or audio c.d. book, they like to make donations. Thank you once again to the people of Chicago. Wooooowww....I just sold another book to this man and woman. They asked me would I remember them when I made it. They laughed it off saying, "Of course you're not." I returned to my seat and before the man went upstairs he offered me the second half of his Quizno's sandwich and a bag of chips. Sir...you will be remembered. Dr. Leodis F. Scott, Thank you sir for just being you.

May 19th

Wash day...I usually wait until Saturdays to wash my clothes but it gets to a point that I can't continuously flip my boxers inside out. Eventually, I forget which side is supposed to be the clean side (ha-ha). I know, I know...nasty but at least I wash my body.

I'm starting to make more and more contacts with new people. It feels good when someone says, "It is a pleasure to meet you" and I know it comes from the heart.

Let me tell you one of my crazy thoughts: A lot of times my inner spirit doesn't match up with my physical body. That's why I tell people that I do things just to do them sometimes. My body is moving but my spirit is not inside; but when my inner spirit and physical body connects it is the greatest feeling in the world. That's when it feels as though I can do no wrong. That is when my mental and physical is completely elevated. I don't know what the elements is that put me in this frame of mind but that's when everything feels right to me. Those times are far and few but when they come I enjoy them to the fullest.

May 20th

Rough day. I only sold two books but I have seen huge portions of downtown Chicago. I enjoy looking at the architecture of the city. Chicago is a very big and beautiful city. I went to Roberto Clemento High School and Wells Community High School to speak to the counselors about motivational speaking. The receptionist gave me a calendar with a list of all the schools in Chicago which I will start sending out emails first thing Monday. My goal is to build my resume. I want to hit all ground levels and get my name in at least one newspaper wherever I go so when I hit the radio stations I can tell them that I'm being recognized all over. This road takes a lot of patience.

With so much empty time on my hands I continuously write and that is what keeps me strong. I know life is full of ups and downs and I have to enjoy them both equally. Today, I heard a quote in this song, "G.R.I.N.D" by Asher Roth that I would like to share with you because the words hit me deeply.

"It's not about fame and fortune

It's about believing

And believing in yourself

And understanding that this life

Is life

Its liberty and the pursuit of happiness

It's not about getting what you want all the time

It's about loving what you have"

I pray that people are enjoying what they have. Sometimes you just have to play the cards that life gives you. The cards that are dealt to you have to be played to the fullest. Embrace what you have and always remember that there are people in far worst situations than you are in. Sit back and enjoy the days as they come. Life is too short to be stressed over things that you can't control. Step outside your box. Listen to new music, explore one of your ideas, laugh…especially laugh. Humor is the spice of life. Learn how to play a musical instrument, dance in public, sing out loud, smile all the time and most of all; appreciate the little things that life has to offer. Once you stop living you are preparing to die. Mental death is the worst death of all. Don't ever stop learning. Don't ever stop reading. Reading is essential to the soul as water is to the body. Reading unlocks the conscious and subconscious parts of your mind. Most people are a product of their environment and become afraid when they start seeing the bigger picture. Stepping out of that box is scary but that's what true living is.

2nd entry

Dinner tonight was 10 cheetos, two pieces of bread and a half bottle of water. I'm just happy to have something to put on my stomach. My friend said that it looked like I lost about seventy five pounds. Maybe so. Up here I have to cut out the drinking because I'm afraid I won't wake up on time at the self storage unit. Since my "job" requires a lot of walking I am constantly moving, plus the fact that I stay in the gym helps. When I get focused I don't worry about eating. All I can think of is working. I develop tunnel vision and remain focused, but I still get lonely. When I'm in café's I always invite people to join me. Not because I am attempting to get with them but rather because I want to enjoy a conversation with someone. I talk to a lot of people throughout the day but I rarely get a chance to converse. I relish in those moments every chance I can. When I talk to people they usually want to pick my brain on who I am or about my mission. That is all cool but sometimes I want to take off the *Traces of You* cloak and just be Raymond Goode. It's few and far between that I feel like that but when I do, I want to enjoy the moment for as long as it lasts.

Well, I have blisters on my feet and I'm mentally and physically drained. Tomorrow I have to get back on my grind. There is no rest for the weak and weary. Every day I wake up I am blessed to know that I have another opportunity to see another day. I am able to move my feet and arms. I can see and hear. There are so many things to be grateful for.

May 21st

A cold front definitely moved in last night. Since I don't have any covers I had to wrap up in as many clothes as I could. *Pause: I'm used to this by now. Play:* As long as I can wake up to a fresh day, I am happy. All the problems from yesterday are still yesterday's problems. Today, I have a fresh batch of problems to deal with but I am still thankful for those problems because at least I have the opportunity to wake up and deal with a fresh batch of problems.

I spoke to this woman who told me that she was unemployed. I told her that I was unemployed and homeless. She took a step back, looked at my nice clothes and iphone, and was astonished. I told her that my dad's catch phrase is "Never let them see you sweat." I only had three dollars to my name but I am clean, well dressed and properly articulated. Even when I'm down it looks like I'm winning (thanks Charlie Sheen). When she heard the word homeless she said she wanted to help. She said that she knew someone who had a big house and that she would talk to them about getting me a room in their home. I don't ever get my hopes too high but if she helps out, I would greatly appreciate it.

The quote of the day is "Never let them see you sweat." When you wake up; put on your best outfit, style and brush your hair, and hit the streets. Sometimes you just have to see how the day is going to turn out. Don't be afraid to ask for what you want. Surprisingly you just might get it. You can make being turned down into a game. I like to see how many times I hear a "No" before I get a "Yes." I like seeing the creative ways people turn me down. There's the classical "put your hand up" and keep walking, the "No thank you" and I really love the "how much is it" as they rummage through their pockets pretending that they have money. I wait until I hear them say "I don't have fifteen dollars" before I tell them that I have audio c.d. books for five dollars. That's when they tell me that they're broke. Oh and let's not forget the "not right now's" or "Not today." Those are my favorites because I think to myself "When?" I mean its Chicago...what's the chances I'm going to see you again. Overall, my favorite phrase is "Yes...let's support this brother." I have to go through so many "No's" to get a single "Yes" but I don't mind. I just keep it light and fun. I smile the days I make 100 dollars as well as the days that I only make 10 dollars. The thing is to keep smiling...never let them see you sweat.

May 22nd

It's Sunday and what a beautiful day it is. I woke up this morning with no direction of what church I was going to go to, but somehow I was lead to Greater Union Baptist Church led by Pastor Willis. Pastor Willis is a really good guy who asked direct questions. He asked me about my relationship with God. I didn't know how to answer so I fumbled my words until it hit me that I should just tell the truth. I told him that my relationship with God was very good but I was spiritually lost with religion. He completely understood. I enjoyed the direct line of questioning because he wanted to know about the man first and the project second. Then, when we started conversing he was very intrigued on the mission that I was embarking on. I told him that even with me being spiritually lost somehow *Traces of You* continues to bring me back to the church. I know I struck a chord in him because he spoke of me often during his service. I remember him telling the congregation about kindred spirits. He said "Ray and I have connected even though we have never met before."

After service we sat in his office and talked. He was very interested in the fact that I left my three counseling jobs to pursue this mission. He was very interested in the fact that I lived in a self storage unit. I told him "Pastor; my dad said never let them see you sweat. I have three dollars in my pocket but I'm dressed like I'm doing well." He laughed and told me that he couldn't let me walk around with three dollars in my pocket. He bought a book and added an extra five dollars. He asked for a business card and I told him that I only had two left and was trying to save them. He told me to give him one and that he would get one of the sisters to make me some more. Any blessing that comes my way, I'm thankful for it. I managed to sell three books today so all in all I think it was a very good day.

A couple of people ask me to explain how I am able to keep my clothes pressed. First of all I have an iron in the storage unit. I pull out my blow up mattress and stick two composition books on it. I iron one part of my shirt/pants and move the composition books down until I'm complete. I still bundle up in clothes because I don't want to spend money on a blanket. The clothes serve the same purpose as a blanket; keeping me warm.

I went grocery shopping today so I can tell you what I eat throughout the week. I bought three cans of sardines, two bags of chips, granola bars, one loaf of bread, two bottles of water, four pieces of meat, and four slices of cheese. Everything came out to roughly twelve dollars. This will last me until the end of the week. I still grab my condiments from Panera bread. Their free cups allow me to take advantage of their drink selection. I've grown quite fond of Pepsi with lemons in it. And, I still ask for a bag of chips even when I don't order any food.

While writing on my thriftiness, I must add that I only paid for one month at the gym, Xsport which was paid during my first visit to Chicago in January. From January until this day, they have not asked for a second payment and I surely don't plan to give them a reason to. As previously stated, I still leave the storage unit as early as possible and come back as late as possible. "Out of sight, out of mind" is my motto.

Let me reiterate what I said at the beginning of this book. My entire life people have always told me that there is a mark on my life; they say that I am destined for greatness but I am running from something, or that there is something different about me. I can't view myself how other people see me, but I wanted to test that theory. That is the reason why I stripped everything away and entered the world head first. If God has put favors on my life then I willingly open myself and will go in any direction that I'm directed to go in. I tell people that if I die right now then that is the way my life is supposed to go. When it is time to go, I fully accept my fate. I'm not afraid of death because I know what living is. Don't get it twisted…I don't want to die but I'm telling you that I'm not afraid. A mental death worries me more than a physical death. To know what true freedom is and be reverted back to a slave mentality is the worst death of all. Everyday is a new adventure. Everyday I continuously remind myself that I'm in Chicago. Every time I see a new sight I think to myself "I'm in Chicago." I didn't come here because of a job or military orders. I came here on my own free will. I am fourteen hours away from home and as crazy as it sounds I have the entire city backing me. I'm so far away from home that I'm in a different time zone (ha-ha). Tomorrow's a new day full of infinite possibilities, new sights, different faces, happiness and disappointment but either way it goes I will be in Chicago enjoying every moment of it.

May 23rd

I was talking to the editor of G and G magazine (Mrs. Coleman) who told me that she was proud of my success. She said that I was a modern day Moses. I told her that even if I agreed with her I would never think of myself in that light. I told her that I stay humble and play my role. I know there will be a lot of recognition that comes my way, but I continuously listen to that voice that says "You are only a man."

2nd entry

Today I met the editor of BeanSoupTimes, Toures Mohammed. He was very interested in my message and responded back quickly. He told me that he will feature me on his online radio station. I liked his promptness. It will be my first live interview and I am looking forward to being on his show. When I finished talking to him and left out the building I got that intuition that I shouldn't be in that area. I realized that I'm in Chicago and I have to watch my surroundings at all times. I try my best to blend in but it's evident to me that I don't, so I know it's evident to everyone else.

I overheard this guy talking on the phone to his girlfriend telling her that she should skip a day of school because he had been hustling all day and he didn't feel like looking after the kids. Damn…a person trying to better themselves and here he is being her downfall. Then, there were two females getting off the bus and another guy tapped me and pointed towards their asses. I don't know if he felt as though that was the connection that we should have between us but I nodded and continued to look out the window.

There are so many things wrong with the community that it's hard to know where to begin to start change. As I said before; when there is one problem there are at least ten solutions. I hear so many people talk about the problems in this world. They talk about it in seminars, conferences, barbershops, buses and in their one on one conversation, but no one works on the solutions. I want to work on the solutions because I feel as though my life needs to promote change. I tell people that *Traces of You* is merely a book but the dream is so much bigger. As much negative stuff that I've seen I still see the good in people. As a matter of fact that is the first thing I see when I meet people. I remember a teacher saying (on the first day of school) "You all have a 100 A+ grade. It is up to you to maintain that average." When I meet people I believe that they are all good and it is up to them to prove me wrong.

One of my gifts is that I don't just hear people but I listen to them. People will talk in circles but eventually they get to the core of their soul. It is my job to capitalize on what they say and help them hold on to that moment.

As all these thoughts run through my mind, I look out of the window and see kids playing on the school ground. They are so full of innocence and not a care in the world; all while being surrounded by curse words, junkies, prostitution, fights and death. They see and absorb these behaviors in their subconscious. This becomes a part of their everyday lives until they grow and become the person sitting on the bus having the same thoughts that I am writing about. My heart is saddened but I continue on my mission. This is what people call a struggle.

A struggle is not supposed to be easy…that's why it's called struggle. I am a firm believer in the words of my ancestors. My ancestors did not hang, get lynched, burned, castrated, shot or raped in vain. My ancestors gave their best to the world so people like me can have a better future… so *all* of us can have a better future. I refuse to let their dream die. I am a product of my environment because I am a slave to my mind. My mind sees the positive attributes in the people that are lost. Remember that being lost only means that you are in search of something. My mom always said that I can't save the world. Well I'm going to give it my best shot or die trying. I saw this young man get on the bus with his daughter. He is who I fight for. I saw this woman with three kids and studying. She is who I fight for. I saw this guy drinking a beer but turn around and give a little girl a quarter. He is who I fight for. I fight for the very innocence in people because I know it's still there even when it's disguised by ugliness.

3rd entry

Wooooow…what a day! It's been a really good day; besides the fact that I will be on BeanSoupTime next week. I also got a phone call from Urbanviews newspaper in Richmond, VA. They are ready to run my story. That will officially become the third publication that I've be in. I'm making a lot of headway in Chicago, as well. People are starting to listen to me.

I had to take some time out to myself tonight. I needed a beer, some smoke, and some good music. I had to disconnect from the outside world and actually pat myself on my back. *Pause: I have to do this from time to time. Play*: I found out that the storage unit has six floors and a fire escape that leads to the roof where I can see the entire city. This is probably the most beautiful spot I've seen in Chicago. I can see the entire city from one of the worst parts of town. Beauty is definitely in the eye of the beholder. If you get a chance come and check it out. *Pause: I hope I just made this place famous. (Ha-ha) Play:*

Richmond, stand up! I told you that you would have someone to rally behind. I hope that I've shown you all how to do it. Just be yourselves. *Pause: I am feeling really good right now. Play:* I talked to this guy today and told him that my life is going the way it's supposed to go. If I slack off and do nothing then that's how the day is supposed to go. If I sell out of books then that's how my day is supposed to go. If I die right now then that's how my life is supposed to end. I stay eerily calm about my future and what it holds. I'm ready. All I have to do is stay focused and keep my eyes on the goal. The world will see the shine. As long as I remain me, then there is nothing that can stop me. No one calls me crazy anymore. They are seeing my plan unfold. They are seeing what I saw a year ago.

You know what also feels good? *Road to Oprah* is almost complete. In two days I am finished. I have come to terms that every beginning has to have an end. I am sad that this book has to end but it's time to move on to the next chapter of my life. I have to know when to cut it off. My goal was to end when the show ended. I have to stick to my program. It's what makes me...me. I'm ready for the next wave.

I was telling people that my next stop is Atlanta, but I'm making moves in Chicago. I would hate to leave while the skillet is hot. People are listening. I have a message and people are listening. I keep thinking that I just have to hold on a little longer. People want to know why I've come so far to tell my story. I'm ready to talk. Put me on the radio and I will talk. *Pause: Please go listen to Maxwell's Ascension. He is rocking out right now to "Don't ever Wonder." Play:* This has been a long time coming; I promise to do my best. I will put my best foot forward. I want to make my mom and dad proud. I want to make my family proud. I want to make my friends proud. I want to make my city proud. I want to make everyone who believes in me proud. I'm sorry I have to say it again...RICHMOND STAND UP. Take a bow...we did it. Mayor Jones it's time to give me my day. WELCOME TO THE RAYMOND GOODE SHOW.

May 24th

Today was the last taping of the Oprah Winfrey show. I was out there but I had the same feeling I had when I was at the United Center. This is her time. She has helped so many people for the past twenty five years that she should be honored in a fashionable manner. I think it would be tacky of me to talk to her while the world simply wants to show her love and appreciation for her services. I could have been me and started yelling out my story when she came out to shake hands but instead I was me and left before she came out. I know me. I know that if I stayed I could have been boisterous enough to be heard, but instead I remained a fan which is the highest respect that I can give.

On a tangent: my friend helped me to realize some things about me that I didn't know or realize until now. Since elementary school, I have been picked on, ostracized, chased and whatever else happens to the "un-cool" kids. Because of my size I was called, "fat fuck" or "roly poly." The "cool" kids used to spit on the back of my coat. I was always the center of the joke such as; "what's the capital of Thailand?"...Bangkok. Then, the "cool" kids would punch me in the balls. I had very low self esteem and did not have a girlfriend until I was 17 years old and in the 12th grade. Simply put, I was a virgin and did not experience my first kiss until the 12th grade. Everyone in school knew me but I had very, very few friends.

My friend pointed out to me that I was not judgmental and I had no problem talking to anyone. She said she finally understood why I'm this way because I used to be on the other side of the fence. I know what it feels like to be at the bottom of the barrel. I felt the ugliness of people's harsh words and was the butt of their jokes. I, in turn, know what it means to have self hatred because that was what was developed. Enough people said things about me that I started to believe what they were saying. I spent enough mental hours in shame and self pity that I developed a tough shell towards the world. Within this shell, lies a scared little boy full of mixed emotions. Inside this shell is a boy still lost in fantasy world and finding out who he is. The problem with the shell is that sometimes the guard is let down and the outside world penetrates my wonderland. It hurts to let that shell down and people turn out to not be who they say they are.

As I said in the beginning of this book "This book is for the kids...plain and simple." I understand what you are going through and I continuously say "Be Yourself." Don't let the world beat you down so bad that you don't know how to bounce back. I will be the first to tell you that you are weird but that simply means that you are unique. I pray that my life and this book give you the inspiration to continue being yourselves. I am still weird and different but I embrace my weirdness. I have taken the best shots that the world has to offer and stood tall against it all. If I have the courage, than so do you. Remember, If you believe, you can achieve. I am a firm believer in that and my Youtube videos have shown that. Do not aspire to be drug dealers or prostitutes. Look inside yourself and listen to that little voice that's telling you to better yourself. Follow your instincts and not the crowd. Have a tough shell towards the world but continue to live in your wonderland. Don't be afraid to let your guard down but choose when to let your guard down. Letting it down does not make you weak. It only means that you are still human. I am proud to be a fan of the _____ _____ (insert your name) show. I am your biggest fan.

May 25th

Where to begin? My mom (Lynette Goode) had to endure this mission on her knees nightly in prayer. Mom, I'm pretty sure I've racked your brain enough for this life as well as well as the afterlife. I pray that you have seen your son become a man.

To my Dad (Steve Goode Sr.), you have faults of your own, but you continue to be the rock of this family. I UNDERSTAND YOU and love you to death. You have taught me that even with the ugliness of the world; family should always remain just that…family.

To my brother (Steve Goode Jr.), who has always teased and picked on me; if it wasn't for you being a true brother none of this would have been possible. You did your best to keep me away from the streets. I learned how to analyze the streets by watching you. You protected me even when I didn't think I needed protection. I continuously learn from you and I will always be your little brother and you will always be my role model.

To my sister (Lakesha Goode), who has always protected me from my brother; you picked on me as well, but we always had a special bond. You always knew how to pick me up when I was at my lowest point. You have remained my secret best friend since day one. You better be my best friend since you had me playing with barrettes and cabbage patch kids.

To my best friend (Robert Townes), your friendship has been truly one of a kind. I value every conversation, disagreement or argument that we have ever had. You were the first to see and verbalize the light you saw in me. I think that by far you are the most intelligent brother I know. I am still amazed over the foreword that you wrote for *Traces of You* and *Road to Oprah*. Your forewords will be the only words that grace every book that I publish.

To my aunts and uncles:

Aunt Judy; you're the rock of the older generation as well as the affectionate one. You have always known when to put things in perspective. From you I learned how to organize and keep the family together even when there's confusion. Thank you for all the assistance that you have given me on this Road that I am traveling. Your phone calls were the right words at the right time.

Uncle John-Every conversation that we've had has always allowed me to see the world for how it really is. I still believe in every one of your "Gary tales." From you I learned how to remain silent but deadly. Since you always say "I don't care about the success show me the money; I will make sure you are the first one to see it.

Uncle Melvin-You are the funniest man alive and without even trying. Your honesty and straightforwardness is admirable. I have learned to tell the truth at all times no matter what because the truth is the truth no matter how it's looked upon. The truth will either make people laugh or cry but it remains the truth. We are alike in so many ways. I will keep my new place clean (ha-ha).

Uncle Tony-Each and every time you reached out to family I know it's been from the heart. I learned from you that money means nothing if there's no family to share it with. I learned how to say "No" when it's time to say "No" even when it hurts. I will pay you back all your money with interest…if this dream ever takes off.

Uncle Donald- The straight in your face attitude. None of the traits I learned from everyone else would be possible if it did not end with you. Even with all the caring and affection from the world there are people out there that wants to do harm. From you I learned how to watch the streets and my surroundings. Your teachings have been the biggest parts of me as I go in some of the worst neighborhoods that the U.S. has to offer. When I see a bad group I cross the street. From you I learned how to not be afraid but cautious. But at the end of the day if it has to go down then it has to go down.

To Aunt Joyce, Uncle William, and Uncle Beeboo: I am saddened that you all are not here to see the family as it grows and becomes a tighter unit. You all have produced wonderful children that are family no matter how far or close they are. I learn from your deaths how to live life to the fullest and love at all cost because any day can be your last. I would personally like to dedicate Marvin Gaye's "Got to Give it Up" (Part 1) to all of y'all. That song always makes me think of family.

Let me the first to report to you three that your brothers and sisters are the same and are still living life to the fullest. Your children are a direct reflection of you and your names continuously live in our memories.

It is all of your characteristics that make me...me.

To my friends-I know it's a struggle being friends with me, but that's why I call you friends. You all see Raymond Goode's heart and know that once you cut through the hard shell there is a person inside. I will make sure that you all see your dreams to the end. Even when I'm difficult and you think that I've turned my back on you I will surprise you all. Be patient and you will all see my master plan unfold.

Kids-never ever stop learning, not only in school but in life. Life is a learning experience. I love each and every one of you no matter what you've been through. I love you because you have already been through so much and you are going to go through so much more and the love that is needed needs to be unconditional. Remain an individual and be yourselves at all times. Don't just read *Road to Oprah* but analyze and learn from it. Remember that every moment is a teachable moment.

Margaret Wade-I would personally like to take the time and thank you for all of your expertise and time. You are the beginning of my "University of One" clothing line. Every stitch of clothing that you have assisted me with has brought me closer to me dreams. I remember you saying that my season is now but my season would not be possible without you. Thank you.

To the Media-Remember that I know who I am before I embarked on this mission. I will not succumb to your lies or deception that you will attempt to bring. I will always be me.

To the world-I leave you in the same manner that I left Virginia with and that's with Nas and R. Kelly's, *Street Dream* remix playing.

To Oprah-Thank you for giving me the focus that I needed to complete this project. I found Traces of Me on this *Road to Oprah*.

To Richmond, VA.-Stand up! The curtains are closing on the Raymond Goode show as Goapele's, *Closer to My Dreams* plays off.

TRACES OF RAYMOND GOODE

Website: www.TracesofYou.org

Email: raymond.d.goode@gmail.com

Facebook: www.facebook.com/raymond.goode

Youtube: http://www.youtube.com/GoodeRaymond

Blog: http://raymondgoode.wordpress.com

Twitter: @RaymondGoode